Abrahamson

MW00593371

TEACHER LOVE ME
FOR I AM AFRAID

Gracious Inclusion Series

Kristen Gay –

I'm a testimony to

the power of Gracious

Inclusion!

Thank you for your kindness!

Dan Abrahamson

Danny   (I gave a copy
  ⧣   to
          Emily Bright)

To my Wife:
You have never let cancer or your pain define you.
For you, never thinking of self,
have always reached out to all others first.

CONTENTS

PREFACE vii

CHAPTER 1: *Abe* 1

CHAPTER 2: *Danny* 5

CHAPTER 3: *Winding Roads* 11

CHAPTER 4: *My First Year Teaching* 17

CHAPTER 5: *Fear-to-Love* 27

CHAPTER 6: *Bullies and Misfits* 35

CHAPTER 7: *My Heart is Crushed and Legs are Broken* 47

CHAPTER 8: *Out of Control* 55

CHAPTER 9: *Bald is Beautiful—A Mirror Reflection* 67

CHAPTER 10: *Honey, I'm Home—Money Woes* 75

CHAPTER 11: *Clear the Clutter to Find the Kid...It was Time* 81

CHAPTER 12: *Inclusion—Something Inside Demands It* 91

CHAPTER 13: *Gracious Inclusion...Just Hall Duty?* 99

CHAPTER 14: *Lock Down* 109

CHAPTER 15: *Knowing My Students* 113

CHAPTER 16: *Obstinacy, A Science Lesson* 119

CHAPTER 17: *Stupid* 127

CHAPTER 18: *Crayons* 137

CHAPTER 19: *Magic Seeds* 141

CHAPTER 20: *Why Now? You Have to be Kidding Me!* 145

CHAPTER 21: *Letting One Go...From Shart to Finish* 151

EPILOGUE: *Letters from My "Warm Fuzzies" File* 159

ACKNOWLEDGEMENTS 169

ABOUT THE AUTHOR 171

PREFACE

I never thought teaching would be so hard. I love kids and thought reaching them as a teacher would be as simple as A-B-C, 1-2-3—and with majors in Biology, Chemistry, Earth Space Science, and Education I had all the tools needed to do just that. I was ready. Well, there would be unexpected lessons to be learned. Frustration would morph into anger and become my antagonist to reaching kids as I stubbornly clung to the ways in which I had been taught. Embedded in this dilemma was my fear-to-love. During my childhood, at a time when I was known as Danny, I would experience embarrassment, guilt and shame. Believing love could be lost, and forever separated, I would fear-to-love. This would ultimately give me the impetus to think differently and turn that thinking into action.

Throughout my 36 years of teaching, I became affectionately known as Mr. Abe or just Abe. Teaching and reaching over 7,500 students, including some family next generation upstarts, has been my reward, but in my early years for some—too many—that was not the case.

Grudgingly pushing piles of failing tests off my desk, they sat in a dark corner far away, separated from the rest.

This book reveals Abe's transformation as unresolved conflict from failures in the grade book to failures in himself festers over time. Teaching wasn't supposed to be like this—like a bowl of alphabet soup with crackers clouding the message. Students labeled by others as Train-Wrecks, Losers, Wimps, Misfits, and Bullies seemed to cause chaos where order should be, but letters that float in a bowl of soup cannot be read one at a time. And Abe was trying to find the missing ingredients—the connecter to the chaos; a resolution to the untruths that sought to separate. For the lies that conspired to separate could not stand against the truth that unites.

Lessons learned from Danny, the child, are translated as Abe, the teacher, begins to discover and experience Gracious Inclusion—which would prove to be the missing ingredient time and again. Had it not been for putting Gracious Inclusion to practice there would be no peace. Abe would need to teach from the heart to open the mind.

With this book in your hands I hope that its message can speak to your heart. While these stories come from my experience as an educator, my journey with Gracious Inclusion did not end with my retirement. We all know that lessons learned in the classroom extend beyond four walls. Likewise, this book is about more than teaching—it is about relationships, acceptance, and reciprocity.

Gracious Inclusion welcomes everyone, and it waits to be put to practice.

TEACHER LOVE ME
FOR I AM AFRAID

CHAPTER 1

Abe

"Dumb as a post," Abe fumed, as his uncensored thoughts erupted, splashing out of his mouth onto an audience of empty desks. Abe tried to simmer his temper, but his hope-filled buoyancy for his students' success was sinking into a pool of reality as the weight of each crimson slash slowly pulled him under. The heat was on…

"Dumb, dumber, and dumbest!" One dumb-as-a-post student scored 2/30 on the multiple-choice part of the test. Two right and twenty-eight wrong, not even a guessing percentage. Abe shook his head in disbelief.

They would have to know everything and pick the wrong answers to do this poorly. The classroom had grown cold, so Abe reached for his green sweater inside the closet door. Moving at a snail's pace with only two gears, "slow" and "no-go," by the time he finally finished correcting, one third of the students had failed—*all "Posts,"* Abe thought, and he was lost in the midst of them, *someday someone's gonna take me out of this classroom, but not today.*

Yes, Abe was thoughtful, calculated, and full of intention—each decision had a goal with a logical purpose. He was happy when life was concrete and sequential, like the pattern of his own thinking. Yet these "Posts" were proving to him time and again that what seeped through the cracks of the classroom was a mix of chaotic vapor that had not yet condensed into visible appreciation. Abe had grown impatient, even for a snail.

Off his desk, Abe placed the stack of failures in a separate pile near the waste basket. He did not want this to be his problem, but they could not be thrown out, so Abe physically distanced himself from them as something deep inside caused him to push them far away. They would not interfere with the glory of his moment—the pride he felt as a teacher was in the success of those students who shined. The unwanted tests now sat silently in a dark corner where they belonged. They had been cut from the rest; the same way Abe had isolated Brad years before.

Brad, Abe's five-year-long failed science project, sat in the same desk with a new group of ninth graders year after year doing the same thing each time, which was absolutely nothing!

Abe, the only science teacher for this grade, tried help Brad by pounding the same curriculum into him, but with each blow the Post just sunk deeper and deeper into the ground until it was no longer there. At age 19, Brad finally dropped out of school and vanished, making appearances periodically in the local newspaper under the Sheriff's Report. And, as Abe found Brad there, a repulsive force of unresolved conflict reemerged…Abe too felt sequestered.

Sit, soak, and sour. Posts were just another unopened can of soup that had sat on the shelf too long with its label fallen off. These predictably uncontrollable, unidentifiable entities were everywhere: an unexpected fire alarm, or a bomb threat, a student in the hallway whose face would turn and hide, the classroom clown who was always in Abe's face, some filled with anger, some just plain empty. Pushing Abe's buttons, disrupting his routine, they always seemed just beyond his reach or level of understanding.

Abe gazed out the window of his classroom. The sun had set pulling down with it all the colors of ROY-G-BIV with the exception of a fading purple which clung to the sky—and he, like indigo and violet also stubbornly stayed. For he had vowed never to bring his work home and to always leave the classroom with everything graded and ready for the next day.

All was quiet and then time made its presence known as the ticking from the Chemistry clock hanging on the wall suddenly became loud. It read almost Potassium O'clock, element "19," nineteen hundred hours military time: 7:00 P.M. As if being awakened from a hypnotic state Abe rose out of his chair to stretch.

He took intermission from his mental strain with the mundane task of putting away some Bunsen-burners and wiping down lab countertops. After the respite of this welcome departure Abe returned to his desk to finish grading lab reports.

Posts showed passive aggression by handing-in nothing. Their zeroes in the grade book seemed to be laughing as they tried to ruin his day. The hands on the clock had reached twenty hundred hours, pointing to Calcium, when he finally walked away from his desk. It was time for him to leave the menagerie of chaos behind.

His car stood alone in the empty parking lot. Only grading nights were late like this. And when looking up into the night sky Abe saw the stars and the vast dark space between them and he wondered, *Why? Why am I a teacher?* We are puzzles made of bits and pieces from our yesterdays.

CHAPTER 2

Danny

"Danny, time to get up," Momma called. "It's your first day of school."

"No, I don't want to go!" Danny was worried and had to be pushed to finally get ready. Walking out of the house, he dragged his feet kicking up gravel from the driveway. "Wait Momma, I have to check something in the sandbox," Danny contested.

The sandbox was made of an old wooden rowboat, a remnant from the original summer cottage. Danny fussed over the placement of his Tonka toy road grader. It hadn't finished making its pathway in the sand leading up to the rowboat's bow. "Come on, Danny," Mother beckoned, "you'll be fine."

His voice quivered, "I don't think so." Danny didn't like the notion of moving farther and farther away from all that was familiar to him. He managed to squeak out a farewell to his little sister who waved good-bye from the safe confines of the porch window. She wasn't going outside. She was secure and still in her P.J.'s. But Danny, like a brave pioneer, took a deep breath and continued to move towards unknown territory.

It was autumn and apples had rolled, as they always had, from the tree on top of the hill. They lay crushed on the driveway below. Even this early in the morning bees were already soaking up their sweetness. Fearful of getting stung, Danny walked quickly past them. "I don't like them bees!" He grunted.

Momma held his hand, "Oh, just smile at them, Danny, and they won't hurt you." Well, he smiled all the way to the big boulder rocks where his older sister was already safely sitting.

"Here's your spot." His sister pointed to where she wanted Danny to be. "Sit on the nice flat rock." The rock felt cool and from there Danny could see the mailbox covered with white-striped, blue morning glories that had opened their flowers to greet the rising sun.

Soon Danny heard the vehicle that would take him away. It was an orange box with wheels and had brakes that squeaked. As the bus slowed to a stop the door opened like an accordion and Danny, following his sister, took his first big step.

The bus driver who was a retired pastor, greeted them. "Good Morning, I'm Mr. Rustad." Timmy, who lived on top of the hill by their church was saving a seat for them. Mom blew a goodbye kiss, and then it was off to school.

Danny's class of sixteen stood in a circle all facing each other as they sang "Old McDonald had a Farm." Miss Latt, Danny's Kindergarten teacher, then taught them two new songs called "Big Eyed Rabbit" and "All Night, All Day." Soon song time was over, but time had also run out for Timmy because when Danny looked across the circle, a pool of yellow liquid lay below the feet of his pee-soaked trousers.

"Oh, no!" Timmy looked down at his wet pants. Everyone stared. Timmy appeared lost, so very far away and separate from our group. Danny felt his face redden in embarrassment for his friend. The square shaped Elgin clock on the wall moved slowly. Time seemed to stand still—a problem for Timmy that Danny could not fix.

By noon, half-day of Kindergarten was over and Mr. Rustad was driving Danny home. As the orange bus slowed, he jumped out of his seat and proudly announced, "That's my house!" The same squealing brakes that had warned of his departure into the unknown now celebrated his safe return.

Jumping off the last step of the bus, Mom caught him in her arms. Walking up the driveway, hand in hand, they looked at the bees feasting off the fermentation of crushed apples. The bees were too drunk to fly. Smiling at them bees Danny asked, "Momma, do you know what happened to Timmy today?" No longer smiling, he told her, for Danny had learned a lesson in Kindergarten, and his friend had been stung.

●●●

Memories wrapped in emotion, this story about Timmy is the earliest time I can remember myself, as Danny, empathizing with another person's misfortune. Embarrassment had separated Timmy from the group. Why did this have to happen to my friend, or for that matter anybody? Especially on the first day of school. But I could not control nor predict the unraveling of that day's event. In another, I had sensed my own vulnerability.

I look back and see Danny contemplating the meaning behind his day, seeking to find the answers to his worries. Momma tucked him into bed and with eyes wide open Danny looked at the ceiling which had a light that stared back at him. He always said, "Momma, it kind of looks like a wheel on a boat." The light shined through the design of anchors attached to ropes—and so, with a wheel to steer, a boat to fish from, and ropes attached to anchors, Danny had what he needed: control, fun, and security. Then I hear Danny singing to Momma his two favorite songs from kindergarten, which filled him with a sense of safety and security. He was safe. It had been a long day, and Danny was tired. "Love you all the time, Momma."

Momma gave him a kiss, "Love you all the time, Danny. Sweet dreams." Love is reciprocal.

Danny loved his sleep. Screening out all the noisy confusion from the day, he panned for his fortune, and upon awakening Danny looked into the miner's pan, hoping to find what he was searching for—that illusive golden nugget.

Kindergarten was meant to be a safe place, but during play-time, the tower of blocks that Danny built, even when protected, would be knocked over. More tomorrows would come and towers would be reconstructed. And he would take home the lessons learned. Children are filled with resiliency.

In the worrisome struggles of growing up, beyond the limits of my own understanding I loved and was loved to the nth degree—so much I would never know how much.

CHAPTER 3

Winding Roads

Countless mornings I awoke, not as Danny, but as Abe, the teacher who had yet to find any nuggets in the miner's pan. Whether a prospector struck it rich or not, the miner would always be hungry for more, or in Abe's case, at least something that would keep him going—for Abe needed to get back to work. It seemed like Abe had only been gone from school long enough for his car's radiator to cool down and then warm up again.

As Abe traveled down the familiar winding turns of the river road, he drove past Brad's childhood home and driveway where he so often had seen Brad waiting for his school bus. Some days Abe would be caught behind the bus's early route and when he stopped for the flashing lights Abe smiled, for like Danny's old bus, it too had brakes that squeaked. But now, years later all that remained at the end of Brad's driveway was the stub of a broken, weather-beaten, wooden post. And Brad too was out of Abe's life, no longer there—just gone.

Driving to school Abe never listened to the radio. The silence gave him time to think about his lesson plans. They already had been written and lay waiting on his desk. Abe was challenged to try to remember what had been planned— he hoped he would not lose another Post.

When he entered the classroom, the clock showed fifteen minutes 'til Oxygen. Not being an early bird, he had chosen the option of coming in at quarter to eight and staying 15 minutes later at day's end. Abe was never in a hurry to leave but always rushed to arrive. Time moves but tests don't because there they were right where he had left them. The stack of passing students sat close, proudly on top of the desk and pushed far away from these still lay the stack of failures—the sunlight now enlightened a once dark and ill-forgotten corner.

Red is the teacher's preferred color for correcting. Abe had decorated those that didn't belong with a big fat red "F." *That should motivate them to study harder,* he thought. And if that doesn't do it, he would just remind them it's a required class and if they don't pass, they'll have to take it all-over. Once again, a cold feeling came upon him and he reached for his green sweater and then shut the closet door. The stack of failures stared at Abe with contempt and he smacked them with a plastic ruler causing it to splinter. Red can even make a bull mad.

Later that day Abe returned the tests and fired his rehearsed thoughts back at them. Confidently, he smirked as he thought, *that ought to fix it.* A good coach puts a bad loss behind him and so with a clean slate Abe planned and worked hard, giving extra focus to the struggling students until they were ready for the next exam. This time test results would surely be different. They were all going to be winners.

After each test Abe anxiously pulled out the answer key, a measuring tape, which provided him with accurate, calibrated insight regarding percentile rank and knowledge gained.

Danny believed all the pee-soaked trousers of the world could be laundered and reconciliation could be attained, even though as a teacher Abe knew it wasn't true. Nonetheless, he began correcting with high expectations. But, as in a chemical titration, drop-by-drop the stack of failures once again grew and his mood increasingly soured. Correcting another failed test Abe counted, "Wrong, wrong, wrong! Dumb as Posts!" Like drops of vinegar, they disturbed Abe's equilibrium. He would quickly reach the same endpoint.

In the essay part of the test Abe looked at the large empty white space which he had generously provided so students could fill it in with all of their wisdom. This space stared at him, still empty. *Did the student forget to read this page? Maybe the pages stuck together?* No, Abe quickly figured this not to be the case as he flipped to the front page which showed the name of a Post!

With a long red slash, Abe pressed so hard it almost cut through the paper and then circled the entire area, indicating nothing had been written. Abe had learned to do this because once returned, a Post might try to write in the answer and make claim for an error in correcting. A red circle was quicker than going down to the office to make a copy— which was not beneath him to do, in order to catch a repeat cheater who had pushed his buttons once before. Traveling down the short-answer part of the test, red circles linked emptiness together making it look like a chain. Tired of making small circles Abe turned the page, and no longer willing to award the respect of so much time correcting he simply put a big red circle around the whole group of unanswered questions. Dropping the guillotine quickly was less painful, not for the Post, but for him.

On the last test Abe corrected a Post wrote, "Mr. Abe, you know if I knew the answers to these questions I wouldn't still be here." With his red pen Abe wrote back, "Then Stay!"

Overheated, he knew he had to make his way down to the teacher's lounge, a place that he usually tried to avoid for the smoke from the cigarettes was so thick it made the air turn blue and the synergistic combination of gossip and bitching and moaning made it a place that was immediately unhealthy. Abe guarded himself against the decrepit onslaught of satire flowing out from the mouths of those whom he inwardly questioned how and why they had stayed in the profession. Once in a while Abe would enter to avoid the appearance of being anti-social, but sometimes, like a pressure valve, it was needed to prevent him from exploding after a really bad class period or round of correcting tests.

Mr. Cagan, Abe's reason for entering the lounge, was an unofficial mentor and one of his closest colleagues; not that they saw eye-to-eye on everything. In fact, most times not agreeing on anything. "How was I to deal with all these Posts?" Abe frequently asked. Cagan, round and rotund would sit back, rolling in his chair, wearing a half smile and listen to Abe's ramblings from the upstart. No solutions were really made from these conversations, but Cagan had been around for a long time and seemingly was not shocked, knowing this was just part of the territory. Abe felt better, but knew it was only a temporary appeasement.

Coming out of the teacher's lounge, Abe always smelled like an ashtray even though he never touched the cancer-sticks. Yet Abe's students believed the gum he chewed hourly was laced with nicotine even though he showed them it was cinnamon flavored Dentyne to offset his dry mouth from his medication.

The next day the smoke from the teacher's lounge still permeated his green sweater, lingering, as did Abe's unresolved conflict for what to do with these Posts. Abe dumped the miserable news into their laps and threw out a demand, "Study, study, study!" And then added a stinger: "You just don't want to learn. Maybe a phone call to your parents will help!" But telling that to a sixteen, seventeen or worse yet eighteen-year-old was like giving them a squirt gun to put out the fire that was ablaze in their home. And Abe knew he wouldn't be telling their parents anything they hadn't already battled.

Who was teaching whom? He thought. The emotional current swept Abe far away from any condition for behavioral change. The analysis was simple as A-B-C, 1-2-3. But he could not separate himself from the situation far enough to see the Antecedent, the frustration of Abe's hope; the Behavior, the Posts doing nothing; and the Consequence, Abe blowing his top. It was crazy for him to be doing the same thing over and over again and expect different results.

As a science teacher Abe should have known better, but Abe was stuck in a cycle, spinning round and round, caught in turmoil, and unable to change his ways. Posts made him feel alone. Abe wanted to say "bye" and not "hi" to a Post. They had turned from each other and Abe once again needed a visit to the teacher's lounge.

Claiming one last breath of fresh air Abe entered and flopping into a chair kicked his feet up onto a pillow and dumped the shit from the day into Cagan's lap, proclaiming, "You know, I really don't need this place."

Cagan slapped Abe's feet off their resting spot, scolding, "You don't do that at home, do you?"

Abe abruptly stood up and huffed back, "You're not my mother!" And he left. For Abe too had been stung and he would carry with him an empty miner's pan.

CHAPTER 4

My First Year Teaching

Mason City was calling me out of the comfortable confines of my home in Minnesota and as if getting on the school bus for Danny's first day of school I was leaving all that was familiar to me. It felt like my foot was stepping on a nail as I pressed down on the gas pedal of my 1978 school-bus-yellow Ford Fiesta.

The lakes, trees, and my family were in the rear-view mirror as I headed south into unknown territory. I wasn't convinced this place would be what Mom called "my new Mayberry." This was a solo trip and the fear of separation overwhelmed me. Crossing the state line was a welcome sign that I read, blurred through tear-filled eyes, "IOWA... A Place to Grow." All I could see growing was miles and miles of endless corn fields. *Where would it have its place for me?* Growing pains hurt.

Roosevelt Junior High was built in Mason City, Iowa before WWII, when it was the pride of the community, originally built as the high school. But now it was sorely outdated and it was on the "wrong side of the railroad tracks." Funny, how first year teachers are given the job that no other teachers in the district want. But I was here now, and ready to see my classroom.

My building principal greeted me, "Welcome aboard." His fingers fiddled with something, not as if wanting to keep it, but to the contrary, more than happy to give it up. My jaw dropped wide open as he pressed the big forged iron key for my classroom into the palm of my hand. I recognized it as a skeleton-key much like the ones in my grandma's turn of the century house. It was smooth and simple. His eyebrows lifted, suspending them for a moment, and tilting his head to the side, as if posing for a year-book picture my boss gave a quick smile that I read as, "Well, good luck." And then he added, "Your door is the first one on the left." Giving me a final nod, he disconnected. It was time for me to go and check things out for myself.

I walked down the wide and stately terrazzo-floor hallway, sensing the history in this place and thinking students, now the age of my mom and dad had their memories here, and now mine would be here too. I had been taught something that was old was worth keeping: age was beautiful, and that in itself gave it purpose. My room was right next to the front office, so even though my mind had traveled a great distance, my feet didn't have far to go.

The old key was put into the lock and I felt the weight of the tumblers turning, making a loud clunk, unlocking memories of my Nana telling Danny about her teaching Botany, 70 years prior, in a building perhaps much like this one. For twenty years Nana embraced teaching, then had to give it up, having her Minneapolis teaching certificate revoked because she got married. She would have been proud of me and now I carried her with me as the two-and-a-half-inch thick, oak door swung open, and I, as Abe, stepped inside.

The air inside the old science lab smelled musty, and on the counters lay 180 textbooks for six sections of eighth graders, who Abe idealistically believed would all be hungry for knowledge. The textbook showed a program designed for independent study where students were to learn at their own pace. There was only one week to prepare.

Students arrived that first day, some walking and some running. But Ricky entered the room on all fours. Getting down on his hands and knees, Abe looked straight into Ricky's eyes and asked in a crazy off-the-wall manner, "What are you dooo-ing?" Ricky cocked his head, paused, and stared at Abe as if he were a rooster ready to pluck an eye out. And then Ricky answered Abe's inquiry…

"Looking for bugs," he mumbled. This was the beginning of the chaos. Still on his hands and knees, Abe asked himself the same question, *What am I doing here?* In what seemed to be one exhausting breath, three weeks passed, and Abe realized he was in a state of calamity.

Each 45-minute class was filled with kids all moving independently in different directions. Some students were already in Chapter 4, while others still hadn't started the lab activities for Chapter 1. All added to the confusion. Some just had worksheets, while some students went up to the library to take their chapter test, and others were just trying to finish (or start) a new lab. The frenzied movement reminded Abe of ants as they scurried about trying to reclaim order after kicking the sand of their hill off the sidewalk. Abe no longer had to wonder why no one else had claimed this job for themselves.

Confusion reigned. Dirty test tubes were strewn about laying everywhere. Every day, Abe felt like quitting. At the end of each day, he went home to collapse on his bed, falling asleep quickly and sleeping so soundly that he melted into the mattress. But as much as he wanted to stay there in the comfort of his bed, he still had work to do. So, after a two-hour nap Abe returned to school and worked until 10:00 P.M. trying to clean-up the lab, catch-up on endless correcting, and prepare new tests for the next round of chaos.

Every morning like clockwork, two students, Ken and Robbie would wait for Abe at the school's front entrance and stick with him like a shadow into his room. They worshipped Abe, but he couldn't imagine why—to himself Abe was such a failure.

Making it to Thanksgiving was a milestone and unexpectedly the Monday after, one third of Abe's class was missing. Migrant workers had moved to more southern states taking their children with them. With fewer students to manage Abe felt that things would now certainly get better, but they did not.

Being a novice, everything was new and every ounce of Abe's energy was used on the simplest of tasks, wearing him out from repetitive frustration. Imminent needs for his students to be successful should have been addressed but went unnoticed. Abe's eyes were open, but his head was up his ass—it was all shit, and he could not see. Eighth graders are programmed to wander and to wonder. But their innate curiosity was viewed by Abe as mischievous rather than inquisitive. Seeing them as animals, Abe behaved as one too.

Abe tried to assume control by bellowing helpful instructions like, "Quiet! Sit down and shut up!" and "Can't you kids stay organized?" Roaring like a lion made students like Ken and Robbie jump out of their seats but did little to change classroom behavior. Sheila continued to throw chalk across the room, Daryl kicked the waste basket whenever getting a failing test handed back to him, and Nelly put a staple through her finger, thinking it should have made a ring by going around it, but requiring a Band-Aid instead. Ken nudged the lab table inch by inch into Robbie's pudgy tummy. Robbie giggled, "Shoots away!" They both laughed. Eighth graders spoke through a channel of emotion that was seldom blocked, while Abe's emotional channel all too often seemed to block his reasoning.

Shoots away… Abe thought, as he rubbed his brow, never thinking to ask its meaning. He figured it must be some sort of code; a release mechanism for the stressors that bump into you throughout the day. Knowing the agreeable students from whom it came gave Abe a half smile.

Nelly came up to Abe for another Band-Aid. Spinning, Abe was bound in turmoil and silently screamed, "Get me out of here!" The bell mercifully rang and for three minutes Abe breathed a sigh of relief.

Gene, Abe's dearest friend—a social studies teacher from across the hall—came over in between classes, put his hand on Abe's shoulder and whispered, "You were really yelling at those kids. You'd better come over to my house for supper, and bundle up, the mercury's dropping out of the

21

bottom tonight." Abe had been adopted by Gene's family. They were his one refuge during that first year of teaching and provided the only times when Abe could feel at ease and be himself.

After school Abe hurried home and then with snow flying behind his car instead of the usual lime dust he high-tailed it down the all-weather gravel road to Gene's house. They had supper, Abe wrestled with Gene's kids, and then they all decorated Christmas ornaments and hung them on the tree. Soon the clock bells chimed, triggering Abe's sense of professional obligation.

It was already 9 o'clock on a school night and Abe felt compelled to go back to his classroom and get ready for another hellacious day. Before leaving, Gene's kids gave him a shoe box wrapped in comic-strip newspaper with a message written, "Open later, Merry Christmas." As Abe left, the thermometer outside on the deck read negative twenty.

Abe pulled into the parking lot. The school was dark and uninviting, and the small flame of warmth inside of him was blown out as he opened the door of his Fiesta. The bitter cold even gave voice to the snow. Its whimper squeaked as the weight from each step under his boots seemed to squeeze the life out of it. The wind and the snow blew, adding to Abe's pain. He didn't know cold could burn and wondered when it all would stop.

While working in his classroom, Abe heard tapping from the outside of the frosty windowpane. It was the seventh-grade science teacher, Marvin.

"Abe, open the front door. I don't have my key," Marvin beckoned. It took Abe only a minute before Marvin was in the building. Walking down the hallway was slippery as the snow began to melt from under his boots. "I was driving by and saw the lights on." Abe thought about being home and Danny looking up at the light that looked like a wheel on a boat with anchors that held it secure. Funny how in times of need Abe would be taken back to Danny.

But now Marvin entered Abe's classroom, looked around, and shook his head. "This place is a jungle, what the heck is going on?"

"Well, see..." pointing to the dumpsites littering the corners of the room, "That's Chapter 7, that's Chapter 8, and over there, well that's Chapter 9 and beyond." Being blinded and battle fatigued, bewilderment had filled Abe leaving no room in his brain for creative thought. Sometimes you can't see the forest for the trees. Abe's lower lip quivered just as it did when his emotions got the best of Danny. Letting it all out, his eyes began to water—Abe was broken.

"This is crazy." Marvin stroked his beard. "Why don't you teach all the kids one chapter at a time?"

"Guess I never felt I had that option." Shrugging his shoulders, Abe disgustingly looked down at the floor and mumbled, "Just trying to follow the book's teaching guide for independent study." No other science teachers had ever asked how or what Abe was doing, and he was too busy and naive to even think about asking for help. Abe had not been in the teacher's lounge once that year. Even as a child, Danny would have known better: not to be isolated. But Abe was alone, trapped against a metaphorical chain-linked fence.

"Let me help you clean up and let's get things in order," Marvin grinned, knowing what to do. Marvin was calm, cool, and collected. He was filled with wisdom—something that had traveled far from Abe.

Oh, how Abe wished to be like Marvin, on autopilot and able to have the time to see the faces of individual student expressions, instead of a single mask worn by a dreadful class whose racket prevented him from hearing the rhythm of the beating hearts within.

Before leaving that night, on the chalkboard Abe wrote, "Everyone open your books to Page 130 in Chapter 7." Tomorrow his class would begin with a new sense of normalcy. Marvin and Abe stepped out into the cold together.

As Abe waited for his car to warm up he opened the shoebox and in the dimness of the car's dome light, covered with pine needles, were two plastic ornaments with a note saying, "We'll go with you." He was no longer alone.

The days of trial would not soon be over, but through experience Abe was on his way. The once pain-staking deliberations of his daily teaching schedule turned to routine and would free up more brain space for different pursuits. With this freedom, creativity found its way to flower in the midst of the cold cruel winter.

Each morning stepping out of his car, the northwest wind bit into Abe's face and instead of yielding to the cold, he began to sing, "The wind and the snow it blows, the wind and the snow it blows, the heat goes into the melting snow, the wind and the snow it blows!" And with each determined step this song escalated more rapidly to a higher key until he reached the warmth of his classroom.

In the lab, students heated snow taken from the parking lot, placed it in a beaker, and torched it from below with a Bunsen burner. The melting snow absorbed the heat, but the reading on the thermometer refused to move, and stayed at the melting point of zero degrees Celsius. Once the last ice crystal had melted, the temperature began to skyrocket. But like the latent heat that was hidden from the thermometer, Abe too would have to wait for warmth to show. And then, singing against the wind, he began to enjoy teaching.

By year's end, this rookie teacher had not quit, but had walked through fire and was being offered a continued contract. Declining the offer, he was ready to teach in Minnesota with a world of knowledge never learned from a textbook, and certainly not from an independent study.

It was time for Abe to head back home, for it felt like he had been gone an eternity, and yet, forty years later, it seems as if it were yesterday. And the phrase "Shoots away" had been imprinted on a fledgling—even not knowing its true meaning, over all these years it has become increasingly powerful. Its stealth and timely appearance amused Abe. It was always there, ready to protect like a submarine floating just under the surface, and periodically as Abe would get squeezed this phrase would surprisingly pop up out of nowhere as he would find himself uttering "Shoots away…"

And now while writing this book I am compelled to find the real meaning of this phrase that I once found so mysterious. I found the origin to be "Chutes Away," a 1970s

25

board game with parachutes delivering care packages to be released over targets on a spinning board clustered with various accident sites. Care packages and deliverance—how apropos. For me, it indeed was. "Shoots…oops…Chutes Away!" At least my guess about it being a "release" was right and this phrase would always be there. Yet it would never grow old or under-appreciated for it was a release to problems that needed fixing. Like "Chutes Away," more discoveries would lie in wait—more surprises were to come.

Before leaving, I returned the skeleton key, which had unlocked the lessons for my first year of teaching. I had felt, heard, and saw an old key working. Knowledge showed its power as the dark mystery behind fear broke into the dawn of familiar loving memories. With Ricky looking for bugs, Ken and Robbie looking for me, and my decorated ornament still holding a special spot each year on Gene's family Christmas tree, we all found each other.

Car packed and, on my way, I left Iowa and crossed the Minnesota state line. Looking in my rear-view mirror, with dry eyes I now could clearly read "IOWA… A Place to Grow.

CHAPTER 5

Fear-to-Love

Abe's collection of plastic Christmas ornaments had grown, and now the day before winter break the last one hanging from the ceiling had been thrown into a box with the others to rest for another year. He had tried to keep the thick cotton strings attached to paper clips from tangling, but it was all for not because that's what they became, one big knot. Abe placed his two special ornaments, which had been taped to the Chemistry clock, into the closet with his green sweater and then shutting off the lights, closed the door.

Abe couldn't wait to get home as time for a break could not have come soon enough. He had made a fresh one-inch cut off the base of the Christmas tree. His children had counted the rings just as his dad had taught him to do years before. Abe thought, *kids and trees mark time.* And now for two weeks, tethered to the wall with some bailing twine, their Christmas tree still managed to stand straight in the bay window. Abe was not able to say so much for himself as he felt like an apple whose core had been eaten, and all that remained were the seeds of grandiose idealistic thinking. He

27

did not know what to do with the unreachable Posts. But for now, he was home, away from it all.

Abe lay on the couch, curled up in a cocoon of soft comfort with the warmth radiating from the wood-burning stove soaking into him. The scent of the freshly cut pine brought him back to his childhood and with eyelids heavy the tree lights blurred as he slipped into his slumber reliving memories that came back to haunt him.

●●●

Danny was a homebody and hated the thought of being separated from his family. Yet each summer he was somehow convinced that going up to camp for a week would be a fun thing to do. No one else in his family had to go, but Danny did.

Love and fear laid next to each other like a magnet, two equal but opposing strengths, attractive and repulsive forces coexisted. The same force that attracts would repel as Danny couldn't have loved or been loved by his family more dearly, nor could he have been more worried about being left behind.

Danny's mom had just finished packing his suitcase and then stuck a piece of white-cloth medicine tape to its inside cover. On the tape she had written, "Remember!!!" With his eyebrows scrunched down, Danny stared at the word. He was a bedwetter and while up at camp had to remember not to drink anything after supper. He slammed the suitcase shut.

Danny took some consolation in that his best friend, Frankie, was going up to camp with him. As the school bus journeyed northward it stopped at various churches filling itself to capacity with kids that were strangers to him. The three-hour ride filled all of the campers with pent up energy and once they arrived, Frankie and Danny grabbed their sleeping bags and hit the ground running.

Frankie mustered a challenge, "Race you to our cabin." Pathways had been cut through the heavy forest of Northern Minnesota timber and the race was on. The smell of pine needles filled the air as branches snapped back slapping towards Danny's face as he kept pace nipping at Frankie's heels. Their cabin was snuggled deep into the woods, hidden at a dead end. It seemed dark even in the daytime.

Danny, gasping for air, conceded. The screen door flew open. "Dibs on the top bunk," Frankie threw his sleeping bag into the air, staking his claim. But victory was fleeting.

Five other boys were already in the cabin. The biggest boy shoved Frankie, pushing him into a corner and spewed, "You're not one of us. Get off the top bunk!" Frankie's sleeping bag was thrown on the floor and the ridicule continued.

"Strip him. We'll teach this kid who gets top bunk." Helplessly, Danny watched his friend get mobbed as they pulled off Frankie's clothes, leaving him only in his underwear. A final warning lashed out, "Don't let 'The Hook' get you tonight."

"The Hook" was a crazy lumberjack who allegedly lost his hand at the nearby sawmill. He had also lost his only son in a drowning accident at the camp many years ago and now sought vengeance. In the daytime, The Hook hid high up in the trees. No one could ever see him, but he was up there spying on his prey below, looking for a weak camper, another victim. And then this nocturnal carnivore foraged for his kill as slivers of moonlight pierced through the heavy canopy of pines. Blood thirsty, he could drop out of the trees at any time.

His story lived in infamy and we knew it to be true because that night our counselor rekindled the horror, telling us a bedtime story: "Just three years ago, on a dark moonless night, two high school kids were 'making out' in a car two miles down the road from our camp. A broadcast interrupted the music on their radio sending a warning to all those in the area. The Hook had lost his mind and had gone on a killing rampage. Terrified, hearing this announcement, the high school boy quickly started his car and put the pedal to the metal. Squealing tires burned rubber. Arriving home, the boy got out of the car and like a gentleman went around to the other side to open the door for his girlfriend. And there, swinging on the handle, hung a bloodied hook."

Our counselor then added, "A new hook was forged out of the earth's strongest metal and now he lives in waiting—for justice had not been served." It was completely silent and then we heard, "Lights out boys and pleasant dreams."

An hour went by and Danny's eyes would not close. Then a scratching noise of a hook cut across his screen window. Slipping down deep into his sleeping bag, there he stayed hidden until daybreak.

The next morning the camp's speaker for the week, Pastor Ron, came into their cabin with the nurse and then told them it was time to be checked for hernias. Danny knew what a hernia was because he had a double one, back in 1959 when he was only six years old. *But hernias at camp?* He thought. *How strange...and why is the pastor with the nurse?* Children can sense sinister intent. However, all of the campers were taught to trust and obey—respect for one's elders was the rule.

Obediently, we stripped down to our whitey-tighties and stood in a circle at the foot of our double bunks, like statues—frozen. And then one by one, Danny heard the command, "cough," as pastor's cold fingers touched our vulnerability. Later that day during chapel time, this same man would tell us what we had to do in order to get to heaven, and then pressing on a nerve he proposed a question which twisted into a warning, "You want to be there with your parents, don't you?"

But actions speak louder than words, for what he had really shown me would be this: people make hell for themselves and then with fear being contagious their hell is given to another. Scars from my real hernia three years before were fast fading, but this new wound would not scar, nor heal, as it remains freshly bookmarked—living in the innocence of my youth forever. Fear, a powerful weapon of control, had immobilized me, and at camp not a word about the boys attacking Frankie or the hernia inspection was ever spoken.

By noon the next day, after a morning filled with activity, Danny entered his cabin and his best friend's sleeping bag was missing. Frankie was gone! No one told Danny Frankie was leaving. He was just gone. Danny felt so alone and could not fix it. Later that night, on a tear-soaked pillow, he cried himself to sleep, awakening from his turmoil in a wet and twisted sleeping bag—Danny had peed. "Frankie," he whimpered, "where are you?" But there was only the sound of silence.

Danny returned home days later and found someone else missing. Frankie's dad had unexpectedly died and the funeral, which he had missed, was why Frankie had to go home. Their friendship would fall to pieces after that. So strong is the need of being connected and so strong is the fear of having to let go. The strength that binds is equal to the fear that separates—this dichotomy perplexed me and I would carry the mystery of this force with me. I was loved and yet still captive.

For years, like pieces of a puzzle pressed into a cast of unhealed brokenness, my experiences had found their place in the instilled belief that Danny didn't quite measure up and at any moment could be eternally separated from those whom he loved. He could be left behind.

How could his young life be filled with so many crimson slashes? It felt so wrong. Teeth had bitten into Danny, holding him down. Danny was told to trust harder, that of which he was not able to do, for he was tired and empty. But instead of conforming, deep inside of him a rebel would grow. For secrets had been kept, never meant to be hidden. But toxins corrode the container that holds it and given time it leaks. Years later Pastor Ron, not the campers, would be the one exposed...exposed as a pedophile.

The violation of trust taught Danny to disconnect by saying, "You fool, you made a mistake by trusting." Breaches of trust, not only experienced at camp but in other areas and times of Danny's life progressively pulled him farther and farther away from the connection of meaningful relationships. You give what you have and can't give what you don't have.

Danny had become wary, and increasingly aware of the fear inside of him which like a candle burned ever so brightly in a dark cave. A cave filled with the lies that had kept him at bay, in a spot hidden by silence. But only for a while, because with each step out of the cave the flame from the same candle would lose its power in the light of day. Fear had done its work in him—but the lies that conspired to separate could not stand against the truth that unites.

The teeth that had bitten into Danny loosened, and a Happy Angry Rebel emerged. Fear had backfired, for he now had something special (which would be viewed by those wishing to control others as being outrageous). It was the impetus and liberty to theorize on his own. To think for himself. Danny yearned to reconnect; to have trust and relationships restored.

Choosing to run to and not from his "fear-to-love," as a college student Danny went back to the camp that he hated so much. He worked there for four summers as music director, giving young campers a song instead of a hook.

It was not until much later that I realized how much healing had happened during those summers of playing guitar for those kids. Danny had broken out of the mold cast for him. And so move the agents of change, as does my debriefing. It is an interrogation that I would have to sort out from within. I would battle with different kinds of trust factors in my own classroom, crying because these things are really never forgotten, but wait to be expressed in the action of the present as I find myself as Abe, the teacher.

●●●

Abe woke from his nap. The roaring fire had softened to a smoldering glow. Opening the door to the stove, he threw a log on the dying embers and thought, *Posts are made of wood.* His students were never far from his thoughts, especially the failing ones.

Abe needed to go outside to think, so he put on his coat and walked down the driveway to the street and turned to look back. The house, covered with Christmas lights which even ran up the chimney, shined brightly off the freshly fallen snow. Abe watched as smoke curled out of the chimney and smiled knowing his family was safe and warm inside. For he was their provider.

Then in that moment Abe wondered, *how would this all be connected?*

CHAPTER 6

Bullies and Misfits

Wielding his brand-new metal Zorro lunch box Danny boarded the big orange bus with brakes that squeaked, venturing into his very first full day of schooling: First Grade. Danny hugged it tightly in his arms as he walked down the narrow aisle, passing the first few seats that were already filled. And then, finding a safe spot next to Timmy, he plopped down, touting the lunch box as if warranting display.

"Wow," Timmy's eyes widened, admiring Danny's prized possession. "Zorro is boss!"

Todd, sitting in a seat behind them, was in the same grade but was a little older than Danny and had already lost his front teeth. He sneered, "That's cherry, let me have it!" Todd hastily grabbed the lunch box and all in one motion clunked Danny over the head with it. Danny's brand-new Zorro lunch box had a dent in it and so did his pride. Todd spit through his missing front teeth, "Now it's a piece of junk." Danny's lower lip started to quiver. Relentlessly, Todd went in for the kill, "Are you going to cry now? Cry, Danny-No-Tie, cry!"

Danny once again sank into himself. In Kindergarten, he had mistakenly asked Todd to help tie his shoelaces, for they had come undone. The "Danny-No-Tie" name had stuck, even over the long summer.

Danny knew the power of tying a label to a name and would know that power to be long lasting. I can still picture Todd's tongue hissing through the gap of his smart-ass smile as he ridiculed Danny's inadequacies. But I would not be the only one hurt by others within the great orange box with wheels. An entire pack can prey on the weak and isolated and the school bus was an incubator holding some bad eggs that had hatched.

At the borderline of the school district, Danny's bus turned around in the driveway of a little red-haired girl who badly needed braces. She had large front teeth accentuating a huge overbite. Every day, even in the winter, the older kids sitting in the back of the bus opened their windows as the bus backed out of the little redhead's driveway and like chickens cackled at her, "Buck, buck! Buck, buck, buck!" She ran away from the taunting clamor and I realized not all driveways were filled with sweet memories such as mine.

My niece now owns the very same property where the little red-haired girl once lived. And every time I go to visit and turn into the driveway this story revisits me.

I hurt for those who have to run from their fear. I wish Danny could have done something for her, but he was little, and bullies would continue to teach him about control, power, and the importance of friends.

•••

Recess should be fun, but not with Benny, the bully of the third-grade playground. Danny usually avoided Benny at all costs and feared being cornered by him at recess against the chain-link fence. He wasn't going to find himself alone near this bully. His friend Joe, a kind sort, was the biggest one in the class and would always provide protective cover when needed.

Danny didn't need a sword, just a shield. Even when Joe wasn't around just mentioning his name braced his insecurities, but Danny believed Benny took special notice any time Joe was gone. Danny wasn't a wimp. He was strong, but he was not a fighter. Friendship was what he had to offer, but not to Benny and today Joe was not with him. Recess soon ended without confrontation and as Danny entered the schoolhouse Benny looked at him and sneered, "Small-fry, I'll be catching you later."

Miss Lundeen was the third-grade teacher. That's Miss— in 1962 there was no Ms., you were a Miss or Mrs. Our two-room schoolhouse had no name, but it is where Danny thought Miss Lundeen lived. Even though he knew Miss Lundeen and his kindergarten teacher Miss Latt were both once missionaries in Africa, Danny still believed teachers were chained to their desks, waiting for their students to return the next day. (Abe firmly believed that his high-school students feel the same about him. They were always shocked to see him out shopping at the local mall buying a new pair of colorful Crocs or filling his car up with gas.)

As Danny and his class returned from recess and settled into their desks Miss Lundeen showed the class some spears from Africa which reinforced vivid National Geographic images of bare-breasted native hunters in jungles filled with lions and tigers and bears. In darkness, fear lay coiled waiting to pounce!

Oh, no, Danny's thoughts raced, *Lord don't call me to be a missionary in Africa, because I'll be eaten alive!*

In that moment, the only thing that saved Danny from the runaway thought that he would be consumed by a primal beast was the sudden biological necessity and urge to go pee. Raising his hand, permission to go was granted. All the while, from the corner of his eye, Danny caught Benny making faces at him.

The creak of old wooden steps trailed behind Danny's wake as he raced down the spiral staircase which led to the basement—whose cement floor always seemed damp. It never seemed strange to Danny that the restrooms were in the basement. That's just where they were.

There was no room in this two-room schoolhouse for them to be anywhere else. Danny's bladder was ready to pop and when thinking about the accident Timmy had in Kindergarten, he was afraid that he would share the same misfortune if he didn't reach relief soon. He flew around the furnace, ducking under the octopus-arm heat ducts, which hung low even for a third grader to limbo under.

Making it to the open urinal of the boy's room, Danny relaxed and now had time to rehearse the poem his dad had shared with him in times like these, "Listen, listen, the cat's pissing. Where, where, under the chair, run, run, get the gun. Awe shucks, she's all done." Danny peed with the pressure of a garden hose as if being pinched between the toes of a hippopotamus—then he heard a thud.

There was Benny, alone with head bleeding, knocked out cold and helplessly lying flat on the damp cement floor. He had run right into one of the arms of the octopus furnace. It is easy to love family and friends but to love someone Danny was afraid of was another matter.

Danny didn't want to approach Benny. Yet there the biggest bully lay on the dark basement floor. And then Danny felt as if a circle had expanded beyond himself. He thought, *Why can't we be friends? If Benny recovered, I could throw him a ball, and Benny would throw it back.* There would be no bully in reciprocity.

Danny looked at the blood on Benny's forehead. Then with anxiety dissolving he reached out for Benny's hand. Danny cried out, "Benny's hurt!" The reverberation was a plea that bounced up through the heating chambers ascending upstairs for all to hear.

Benny then awakened, looking up from the floor at Danny and said, "Got ya."

Danny responded, "Yeah, now you sure do." Foe transformed into friend. Miss Lundeen came to the rescue, but in Benny's eyes Danny had done that already.

Teachers have power, but so do students. Hyped up with excitement, the class was dismissed for an extra-long recess that day, but Danny stayed inside with Benny. He never again would worry about being caught in a corner by Benny on the playground.

●●●

Benny, who really had no friends became a good one to me, and through another I found myself. No level of misunderstanding would keep us apart. There is no conflict in the practice of what I now know and call Gracious Inclusion.

Gracious (kindness) Inclusion (together) is a reciprocal relationship giving new perspective to the phrase "love to the nth degree." The number "n" had become bigger than I could have ever imagined, blowing beyond the understanding in my mind, for it came from two hearts.

Danny, pushing his own concerns aside, made the choice to focus on Benny and not his fear—extending beyond himself to include Benny. Danny had taken himself off center stage. As Danny's concern for Benny became increasingly greater, his concern about the fear inside himself became increasingly less. In Danny's mind, they were one. As an equation, it looks like this:

Danny's Perspective
"n/1" (Benny) x "1/n" (Danny) = "n/n" = "1" (Whole)
Benny is most important; Danny is no longer the focus

And Benny, out of need, saw himself small, and Danny, his hero, became very important. Gracious Inclusion had become a reciprocal unifier—each needing the other they had both become whole.

Benny's Perspective
"1/n" (Benny) x "n/1" (Danny) = "n/n" = "1" (Whole)
Benny himself is in need; Danny becomes his "hero"

Whether it is mathematical or in a relationship, the significance of "big" and "small" share equal importance. Both are needed to make it whole. Gracious Inclusion had created an unlikely friendship where fear was harbored before.

No matter what the number or the need, connecting "n" to its reciprocal will always be a unifying product; just put pride in the right spot. Gracious Inclusion is always a "win-one" equation for in its reciprocity it cancels self-centeredness in exchange for other-centeredness—a conversion not only in relationships, but in numbers. So, get in the game: I'll throw you the ball, and you throw it back. Gracious Inclusion expands.

Thinking back to Danny and Benny I realize the teacher was in Danny, the child, and that Danny was in Abe, the teacher. And more bullies would be found, separated like Benny and Danny, hiding underneath it all for they, too, yearned for inclusion.

●●●

Growing up none of Danny's friends belonged to a clique. They were recluse and gave the air of independence, but they all knew better—they needed each other.

Among the misfits was Billy, a wild sixth grader, who quite fittingly lived at the end of "Wildhurst Trail." Billy listened to no one, didn't play by the rules, and always sat near the back of the school bus, where younger kids shouldn't go. But Danny, appearing as a good little conformist, always sat near the front.

Once seated, Billy hollered for Danny, "Yoo-hoo!" With chin lifted, his neck and spine arched as if a Lone-Wolf was howling at the moon. Billy would not be tethered to a pack. His restless spirit and lack of inhibition drew Danny to him like a magnet, as an invisible force stirred the wee-rebel in him, pulling Danny under—hook, line and sinker. They were not supposed to get out of their seats, but Danny took this as a challenge, and the game of not getting caught was on. And so, avoiding view from Mr. Rustad's mirror, Danny, like a water moccasin, slithered beneath the seats along the murky bottom through the weeds from the day's events that had entangled him. The closer Danny got the stronger the force. The tension of anticipation was exhilarating, and then the line snapped, and he popped up to the surface and found Billy.

"Yoo-hoo to you, too!" Danny exclaimed, as they shared a common ritual in the twisting-of-cheeks. Grabbing each other's jowls, they stretched each other's cheeks like Gumby, twisting them so hard they became warm and rosy. In the rhythm of the flow, Billy and Danny yelled in sync, "Ouch!" and then nodding their heads, they looked straight into each other's eyes and chuckled, "Ho, ho, ho...that was a good one." Billy and Danny had learned to funnel hurt and anger, not through retaliation, but rather through an intimacy that only sixth-grade boys could conjure.

So quickly, time transported us from childhood into adolescence. In the 1960s our high school gym doubled as a basketball court and a stage. Chains pulled the heavy, black, velvet curtains opening the view to a twelve hundred cushioned-seat auditorium. When sitting in the front rows, it was funny watching a game at tennis-shoe level. During school, Danny looked forward to Phy-Ed class because that's when he could see Billy. No one seemed to talk to him except for Danny.

Danny and Billy, seemingly opposite, were two sides on the same coin: rebels, but one showed it and the other did not. Danny was cautious, but Billy got into a lot of trouble. Billy held the record for most swats from Mr. Snicker, the High School P. E. teacher, who used a sawed-off goalie stick as a paddle. Mr. Snicker called Billy, "William." There was no time taken for detention or phone calls to parents—punishment for getting out of line was swift and immediate. Vivid memories are wrapped in the emotion of the moment…I can still hear the words from Mr. Snicker, "William, up front, bend over, grab your ankles!"

Holes had been drilled in the paddle to lessen air resistance, allowing it to swing faster. Bending over, Billy's head drooped to the floor as he awaited his corporal punishment. Time seemed to stop and then the paddle smacked across his buttocks making a loud "crack" causing Billy's neck to straighten and head to lift as if being fired out of a cannon towards the onlooking class. Billy could howl for Danny, but for Mr. Snicker there was not even a yelp, nor the slightest whimper. This lone wolf was tough and lived to show it. And now with his shoulders back, chin held high, and face red as a tomato, Billy fell back into the ranks of the class.

Billy was poor and it seemed everyday Mr. Snicker would search to find something that was wrong with Billy. As the class stood at attention for attendance Mr. Snicker noticed a small hole just below the collar of his tee shirt. "Hey William," Mr. Snicker snickered. "What's this?" The gym teacher put his stubby, fat finger in the hole twisting like a corkscrew as if seeking to pierce Billy's heart and then slowly pulled down, tearing the shirt off, leaving a red mark from his fingernail running down Billy's naked chest to his belly-button. Billy never flinched. His face posted no expression. All that remained was the collar of his tee-shirt, two sleeves, and Billy's unwavering pride. On stage, Danny stood with Billy and looked out to an empty-seated auditorium and Danny wished for it to be filled with an audience of witnesses. Teachers can be bullies, too.

Going home after days like this Danny was fired up. And Billy seeing him enter the bus called out the familiar "Yoo-Hoo," which seemed to say, "Come with me, return…it is time to exchange our tears with laughter." By this time, they had grown older, and Danny sat with Billy in the back of the bus. Yet not too old, for it was with a twist and a pull that Danny knew Billy and had felt his pain. With rosy cheeks they were made whole and would continue to celebrate togetherness by proclaiming, "Ho, ho, ho, that was a good one!" From out of the shadows of yet another cave, they had regained control and stepped into the sunlight.

Over the years the big orange box with wheels had provided no place to run or hide. It was a holding tank where kids entered and with a pressure cooker of energy came out changed.

•••

I had been given a gift—wisdom, of which I, as a teacher, had yet to learn how to apply. For my students had red marks that ran from top to bottom on tests that humiliated and made them believe they were failures. Like Danny being hit over

44

the head with his Zorro lunch box, they were taking a pounding. I knew it hurt when something personal is taken from you and returned as damaged goods. Tests were returned to Posts who wore faceless expressions—tough, conditioned to show no pain. Inside they silently whimpered, waiting for release.

For me, nothing could have been more complicated, covert, or sabotaging than turning a student into a Post. Believing there was no alternative, this had become a necessary anesthesia, enabling treatment, masking the pain—both theirs and mine. By removing a person from their name, feelings were no longer an issue. I could not love a Post, and like Todd who refused to tie my shoes I had given them a label that stuck.

CHAPTER 7

My Heart is Crushed and Legs Are Broken

1980—I was happy to be back home and about to begin my second year teaching. I had found a teaching job in a district next to the one I had grown up in. A new journey was about to begin.

The sunrise touched the trees whose outer greenery had leaves that yielded to yellow, orange and a peek of brilliant red. Birds were singing, waking me as they had done so many times before. And the light that looked like a wheel on a boat was also there, looking down from the ceiling to greet me. I stepped out onto the porch and took a deep breath of air off the lake, an elixir known in no other. Then the toaster clicked. The toaster was old and like all other old appliances, a cloth-wrapped electric-cord dated it, one of my parent's 1951 wedding gifts. One that my mother (even up to 2017) proudly reminds me about, as it still looks shiny and new just as if it came out of the box. All to my delight—for Danny, Abe, and I were unanimous on two things—good things should stay the same, and we hated change that was beyond our control.

Being a creature of habit, Abe snarfed down his daily morning peanut butter toast. He needed to go to work. Hopping into his car, Abe slowly backed out of the same driveway Danny had walked down 22 years ago as a Kindergartner. Apples exploding under the tires made a loud crunching pop and disturbed bees flew around the car. Closing his windows, Abe smiled at them. Stopping by the boulders, he looked at the special flat one that he had so often sat upon while waiting for the bus and listened. No squeaky brakes coming around the bend, traffic clear, his car wheels spun with gravel flying.

The familiar turns in the road brought Abe ten years back to the time when Danny had a motorcycle and would recklessly fly around the turns. Then he was bullet proof, immune from all harm. But now at the age of 27, he knew enough to tell the Danny inside of him to slow down and not move so fast. Lessons not on the road but at school were there waiting to teach him.

After Abe's morning classes, third hour had been dismissed and it was time for lunch. Wrapping up a few things at his desk, he found it quiet. Then Abe felt someone watching him. Startled, he looked up from his desk and there stood one of his students, Katie, right there in front of him. Abe, wishing to thwart the notion that something was wrong, asked Katie why she wasn't at lunch.

Katie's face drooped, casting a distant gaze that went through the floor, but not to be dissuaded. What was on her mind came out. "Some kids are calling me a whore," she tearfully said.

Abe thought about the bullies in his past, being isolated, the fear of being alone, and being on the run. Katie was broken, and he wanted to fix things for her. "You know what they are saying about you is not true." Abe thought about the bees in the driveway and added, "Just smile, those kids can't hurt you. I know you are wonderful."

Katie raised her head up and with countenance lifted said, "Thank you."

Like kindergarten-towers that are knocked over, they can be rebuilt, but it takes more time to build than to destroy. Every day that year, Katie came into Abe's classroom with her chin held high and looked at him with a smile.

Empowering students to believe in themselves leads to meaningful connections and I am reminded that these connections are made one student at a time. My one-year term subbing contract had come to an end. And unaware of the future events that would take me back to my second year of teaching, I would go looking for a job in the neighboring school district.

●●●

Abe talked with the man in the office for 30 minutes wearing his finest summer attire—tennis shoes, cut-off jeans and a tee-shirt. He then asked if they had an application form for the science position. "No," the man said shaking his head. "We don't have any here." He then smiled, "I'm the superintendent. Just show up in August. You'll do."

Abe, a protestant-Swede of five generation descent, felt like a transplant in a German-catholic community, which had just opened its first public school in 1965. Living in the next town over, he was a "suit-case" teacher. Good thing he was never asked where he'd be living during his little chat, because small towns liked their money to stay with them.

It would take Abe nineteen minutes to travel eleven miles to get to school from his new home. Down the river-road for six miles and then north for the other five. Coming into town the milk house was on the left across from the "new" cemetery—the old one, at the end of the football field, was next to the church itself and had been filled to capacity for years, long before Abe ever got there.

Abe had grown up just a half hour south of here, but never knew the town existed. For him, the lake was everything, but in this town...well, there were farms. Once crops were harvested in the fall the spreading of liquid manure would smell so badly teachers had to shut the school's windows if downwind.

One of the biggest fall events was getting out of school early for the homecoming parade, which consisted of the band, a homecoming sledgehammered beater car, a few children on tricycles, and a new teacher who carried a sign with two-inch letterhead advertising his arrival. Abe was told that all newcomers had to march—and Abe (who students thought looked like Tim Conway) was the first teacher to be so gullible to believe it and then to actually do so. But Abe was a show boater and after learning about the conspiracy, he joined with the instigators in a good laugh. Never before had there been such a ploy, or ever after would there be. For during every homecoming parade thereafter, he would ask (if and when they got a new hire), "Hey guys, why isn't the new teacher marching?" Abe could make a snake look non-threatening and turn a scuttlebutt into a legend—a gift to others and one he needed for himself. Attention and notoriety; Abe was special.

•••

A lot happened over the next ten years. After buying my new house, I married a woman who, growing up, swore she would not do two things: live in Rockford or marry a teacher. Well, our house is in Rockford, and the second part is a given. More blessings came without anticipation: we had twins and two other children after the doctor said we might not ever be able to conceive.

Happiness, however, can be quickly displaced and being a teacher provided Abe for a greater chance to be acquainted with unexpected grief. You don't look in the obituaries for young people, especially not for a former student. Yet, Katie, age 25, had taken her own life. Abe thought by smiling, Katie would be protected, but now she was gone. She had been stung and he felt like a child where Danny could not control or fix what had been done. The pain of separation, like a nail, once again pierced him. Danny knew the fear a secret could instill, but Abe would never know what was hidden in Katie.

Abe, wanting to go back, was now alone with his thoughts. And he would have to guard himself against guilt-felt feelings that Abe, as a teacher, could have prevented this from happening.

•••

Pain can find many places to hide. Andy was quick with a joke in class and always offered Abe a piece of candy. It was early morning after parent-teacher conferences when a call from the faculty phone-tree awakened Abe with sad news: Andy had taken his life. Abe could not feel his heart beating for it had left him and he was someplace else.

I knew there would be a lot of challenges to being a teacher, but never once did I expect I would be confronted with the death of any of my students. And now it had happened twice—events that were so difficult to understand. Katie had been gone for two years now, and yet, with the news of Andy's suicide, I realized the pain from her loss was still fresh. With my threshold of pain near its kindling point, raw emotions were ready to reignite.

Driving to school, Abe didn't know what to expect. But he knew he had to be there. Abe entered the building and was now in uncharted waters as he saw students hugging each other, hurt twisting their faces. Many had fallen to their knees. It was silent. Abe was not able to make it to his room. He wanted to move, but his legs broke and like a boat filled with holes he sank to the bottom. Ships all around were sinking. Kneeling next to them he cried, "I'm sorry."

"Mr. Abe, are you a minister?" Two students gently asked. Abe did not know them, but he felt their pain and at that moment was instantly connected.

Abe replied, "I feel your hurt and care about all of you, so in that way I am." No other words were spoken.

Grieving was not yet over, for there would be a third time when wounds would be ripped open. Andy had a brother, who a year to the day after Andy's departure, during parent-teacher conferences, took his own life the very same way. The horrific details weigh heavy on my mind. Their bodies are buried in the cemetery next to each other.

Abe took in a deep breath expecting release, but instead every tear cried out, "Chutes away, chutes away," and then for a third and final time there came a diminished and weakened cry, "chutes a…" There was no release—Abe had been left behind. He would have to stay as the pain, filling him with nail holes, left him empty. Two brothers and a girl named Katie were gone.

Teaching wasn't supposed to be like this.

•••

It would never be the same. In an institution set apart for knowledge, love showed its power at a time when pain cut deeper and then deeper still. A welder's torch cuts as it mends—to know the fire that separates is to feel the heat that unites and in this we were one. Sensitive to need, I have reason and purpose for getting out of bed, for I must go to school. My students need me and I need them. Mended with scars that are not seamless, Gracious Inclusion had left its mark.

Abe would carry on and from this point forward teach from the heart to open the mind. His classroom would be a place where love and knowledge meet.

So, teacher love me for I am afraid.

CHAPTER 8

Out of Control

Abe liked his routine. He knew what was best and had guarded against the waves of disruption, escaping that which was beyond his control by doing what he had done for years—teach. He could count on the school bells to tell him when to stop, when to go. Bells were regular and trustworthy, fitting comfortably into his M.O. Teaching was his autonomous utopia: being one of two science teachers for the whole high school he did what he wanted, when he wanted. But now, outside the classroom the tide would turn.

•••

The ringing in my ears started immediately after the fall. A slip, slide and smack into a slab of concrete, stars and lights burned into the eyes of my brain like a hundred camera flashes breaking the darkness of midnight. The tinnitus was relentless, twenty-four seven, robbing me of my sleep. It was a bulldog that had found a bone that it would not easily relinquish. Control was once everything and now I was losing it.

55

The months turned into years and with each passing night a thief slowly stole my hearing from me. Not completely, just in the upper frequencies where my brain heard the tinnitus, leaving just enough hearing on the shelf to keep me in the dark and unaware of what was really happening. My reaction to this insidious robbery was everything but coy. It made me hyper-acoustic, intolerant of even the mildest of noises, from which I tried to run.

The sun was baking, and I was a frog on a hot tin roof with no pond in sight. When falling to sleep or waking up, in the penumbra where light meets the darkness, nerve endings pricked pin-like sensations into my feet. My brain, telling me to run from the unknown, translated fear into what now totals over two hundred seizures—bound in turmoil, convulsing me into fetal shaped contortions, and leaving me spent in twisted sweat-soaked sheets. The diagnosis was Post Traumatic Stress Disorder and the EEG's and video monitoring at the Mayo Clinic's Brain Research Center classified the seizures as "PNES: Psychogenic Non-Epileptic Seizures," a manifestation of my chronic distress related to the head injury. But the loss of control was what I really feared. All the while, my wife Kris remained steady, rising above the white-capped waves, never tossed by the raging turbulence…Kris my wife, my beauty.

During one of my therapy sessions, my psychiatrist said, "Dan, your brain is dying." An awakening that presented with it a conundrum: how could my heart be beating, but my brain be dying? At this intersection my PTSD was trying to put my brain in a tomb. Self-analysis—a time to view myself as Abe. Abe was me alright, but sometimes he didn't want to be there.

●●●

Over the years the climate would change—stormy weather was not the exception, but the rule. Under the clouds Abe continued to teach, for routine was his protective bubble, giving him a cushion against this onslaught of disturbance. But he could not learn anything new and trying to remember his students' names was like swimming with an anchor.

The controlled are the controlling and the controlling are the controlled and that was Abe—a worrier, unable to let go and believe that things would be alright without his intervention. Abe, once again aware of his fear, would have to fight the familiar feeling that held him captive.

Independence would continue to be taken from him by more trauma as a series of events would try to separate Abe from the one he loved. Surrendering to change was like trying to loosen a rusty nut that did not want to turn. But in the midst of battle, Abe would be disarmed and he would have no choice but to let his guard down and start to think differently. The focus would shift and no longer be just about self.

●●●

September 16, 2011: the text read, "Yes, yes, yes." My wife had cancer in all three biopsied areas. Visiting with the oncologist he explained that both breasts would need to be removed along with several lymph nodes. Doctor "T" looked at us and explained that after the mastectomy, breast implants would eventually follow the expanders. Then I opened my big trap, "Then she can be beautiful again."

In that moment, I felt castrated—and before the glare from the doc reduced me to the level of a Neanderthal, I recanted. Beauty was not a pair of breasts. Kris's cancer was growing so quickly that chemo needed to be started immediately, before surgery, and then she would finish with radiation treatments. And so, Kris was poisoned, cut, and then burned, and through it all, I looked into her eyes, telling her, "You are my Beauty, and always will be." That's what love looks like.

4:04 A.M., I am awakened by an unidentified disturbance but do not move. Groggy, the turbulence roars. As the alarm beeps for a second time, realizing it is the sound of running bath water, Kris calls, "Dan, time to get up." It was time for yet another surgery. Threatened by the loss of any perceived sense of control, I was falling to pieces—out of pain, original thought would come, giving birth to my enlightenment. And with no option, I would have to put trust in another.

We had just spoken to the anesthesiologist, Kris was prepped, and I had just given her a kiss. At the very moment the nurse started pushing on the gurney that would move her to the O.R., Kris grabbed my sleeve as if she had forgotten to turn off the stove at home and commanded, "Wait!" And now I, being even more perplexed then worried, looked at the nurse as if we were walking on thin ice and had just heard it crack. Then Kris asked for something beyond my level of reasoning, "Dan, do you have my phone?"

Feeling the drugs were starting to work in her, I shook my head, not wishing to honor such an ill-timed request, and I pushed the phone down deeper inside my pocket next to her wedding ring. "I need to call Marilyn at church..." Kris emphatically explained, "...and tell her the Christmas lights are under the stairs. She will never find them."

Wishing for her return to reality, I cut through the fog and asked three questions that went back to the time when we were first married. "Who loves you, honey?"

Holding my hand Kris responded, "Danny does."

"When?"

"All the time," Kris tried to squeeze me tight, hanging on for the last question.

"How much?"

Kris drifted, with eyes now half closed, she smiled, "So much I'll never know how much..." I gave her one more kiss, and then with love carrying us to the nth degree, I saw her being wheeled away.

Two years had passed since the text message and Kris had gone through six surgeries. And in the midst of the storm she would tell me, "Teach," knowing that was what I needed.

Abe, the king of all worriers would always think the worst, putting Kris in the coffin hundreds of times, but she always had a key to get out—her sense of humor. She even wore a T-shirt saying, "Yes, These Are Fake, My Real Ones Were Trying to Kill Me."

Thinking he had to take care of her, through his own insecurities Abe would say, "Honey, you're going to be

OK…" But before he could take another breath, Kris would give her knee-jerk response, "I am OK."

Life seems to be a riddle, and Abe was lost deep in the woods. So, how far can one walk into the woods? Halfway, then you're walking out. Hell is hot, don't stop—just keep walking because you never know when you're at the halfway point.

Five years later Kris's cancer metastasized. We had waited 34 years to go to Hawaii. We asked Dr. "T" when we should go. He said, "Go now and then go again."

While in Paradise, one night, at 2:00 in the morning I lay in bed next to my beauty, crying, worried there might not be "an again." Kris woke up, held my hand and whispered to me, "Don't be afraid. I'll always be with you." With that I fell back to sleep.

Kris was my teacher, giving me three lessons I would bring into the classroom: live in the present, think of others before yourself, and nothing is so bad that you can't laugh at it—don't let it define you. We both came out changed, as trauma gave way to new and different thinking. And yet, Abe still looks at Kris and wonders what would happen to him if she ever lost that "key."

●●●

May 19, 2014: Kris's birthday, and she would soon be on her way to meet my mom, sister, and niece for a lunch at a fancy establishment a few miles from my boyhood home. But for me, my twenty-minute lunchtime was over, and fourth hour class had just trickled in—it was time for a review.

Abe's curriculum was well established and they needed to get down to business. Funny how each class takes on its own personality. Fourth hour was one big mouth and liked to yak. It was springtime, and in their own minds, they were already gone for the summer. Ready to hold court, Abe threw out a summons, "OK people, listen up." A rumble of thunder was heard from outside the window, but Abe continued, "Test tomorrow, let's get started." And then the storm began as darkened clouds opened, pouring out rain as waterfalls, and windows shook. Abe pointed to the smart board, "This is the real important part." He turned and saw notebooks yet unopened. And that's when his world started spinning.

Abe grabbed the lectern with both hands, his feet planted far apart, and then listed like a rum soaked sailor. The class became silent, and in their silence, he could feel their fear. They were soberly aware that they were in a ship being rocked to and fro by waves trying to toss their captain overboard. They gave Abe their energy, as all eyes focused like lasers, tethering him to the main mast with a sail that was being ripped and torn.

Never losing contact with the floor, Abe's feet shuffled towards his desk. Only two arm lengths to travel but it may as well have been the width and depth of the Pacific Ocean. All in one not so graceful movement Abe partially fell into the wastebasket catching himself on the corner of the desk. He finally spun, flopping safely into his swivel chair. Abe's fingernails tried to bite into the desktop and cold sweat seeped from his pores.

"I'll be alright," Abe said to his crew but more to himself. "Just, give me a minute. I'll be fine."

But Lexie didn't see it that way. Her thinking was on the high road, disconnected from the emotional tar pit that now had captured Abe. She was cognitively aware of the situation that had become questionably dangerous. Lexie calmly stood up and shook her head saying, "I'll be back. I'm getting the nurse."

In the moments that Lexie was gone, emotions overwhelmed Abe, and like frames clicking through an old reel-to-reel projector, the pages of a short-lived movie from his past flashed: *Was it his heart? Another stroke? A panic attack, or was it a haunting from his PTSD?* Fear had frozen him and Abe could not walk. Lexie returned with the nurse and parked a wheelchair so close that it touched him.

Holding on tight to the nurse's arm, Abe stood up, turned, and collapsed into the vehicle that would carry his carcass away. As they rolled him out, Abe guarded against looking into the eyes of his students, choosing instead to focus on the pictures, posters, and poems decorating the walls of his classroom, thinking maybe this would be the last time he would see them. Then he thought of Kris and using humor as a cover to his fear Abe lifted his arms and laughed saying, "Argh, see me in the nursing home!" He felt as if he was being pushed off the gangplank. Disconnected, no measure of pixie dust could help him now.

The bell rang, unleashing a flood of kids from the second lunch period. The small high school that Abe once knew had quadrupled in size. A sea of flounders filled the corridor making Abe self-conscious. He was supposed to be strong, but now they saw Abe being escorted by the nurse rather than gingerly walking down the hallway in his colorful Crocs. Embarrassed, like Timmy in pee-soaked trousers, Danny wanted Abe to be invisible.

Mercifully swallowed into the belly of the whale—the quiet refuge of the elevator lifted him up to the second floor as time for a moment stood still. Then wheeled down yet another corridor with hundreds of students swimming by, there were no secrets here—Abe was not able to hide his vulnerability and he felt as if on display.

In the confines of her office, the nurse checked Abe's vitals. His principal, Bill, had even come down to see if he was okay. Abe instructed that there was no need to call an ambulance and that he would call his wife to take him to the E.R. instead. Grabbing his phone, Abe gave Kris a jingle and began with a phrase that she hated, "Honey, I'm OK, but..."

"Dan, I just went around the 'S-curve'. I'm turning around and will be with you soon." Kris's voice soothed him, "Love you."

Stretched out on the cot, Abe waited, and closed his eyes thinking about the curve where in 1957 his two-year-old sister fell out of the back seat of daddy's car into a mud puddle. The very same curve, where in 1970 a seventeen-year-old Danny laid his motorcycle down, sliding across the pavement. Indelible memories etched in stone, twisting and turning on a well-worn pathway—travel on a road long enough, and familiar twists and turns become dangerous. Now, in 2014, Abe had fallen and was sitting in his own mud puddle. With his world spinning in double vision he needed to keep both eyes closed. So, lying on the cot, he wondered where this new pathway would take him.

●●●

It took Kris 45 minutes to get to school. The torrential rain had dwindled to a mere drizzle and in the car, I listened to the delayed rhythm of the wiper blades as they started to squeak across the windshield. Another 45 minutes later we arrived at the hospital. The rain stopped. No longer spinning, I walked into the E.R. on my own. The medical staff could not find anything wrong. But I knew better and so after being released we drove across the street to my audiologist. It was 5 o'clock and closing time, but not for me—my doctor took me in, as if it were a ready-made appointment. She ran a hearing and eye movement exam, confirming her suspicion of Meniere's disease as being the culprit. Knowledge is powerful and being aware that this had not been a life-threatening episode put my mind at ease.

The next morning, I was still a little shaky so Kris drove me to the place I needed to be, the place that was most familiar to me, the place where Abe was the captain and his crew was waiting for him, ready to sail again.

Fourth hour came quickly and what Abe now said to them came from his heart, "Dear class, I am sorry. Yesterday I scared the hell out of you. I tried to be strong but was not able." In Abe's weakness the class became strong, showing him who they were, filled with compassion, and giving love at time when he was afraid. Abe saw himself in them—for they fix things, and he gave them the following poem:

Radar Love (Illusion of control)

Once it pulled me under— this illusion of control
Down into the murky deep I could not breathe,
see who I was, disturbed in my sleep
Worry, anxiety, frustration bore holes in my soul
Each linked to the other, the chain became heavier
Jabberwockies would not let go

I, in the position of power, must fix it this very hour
But I could no longer tread to keep my head
above the murky waters

The power was in you, to keep yourselves afloat
And with that notion, you stayed in the boat

Knowing what's on the bottom
I will not go down another time
For you showed me
That I am just fine

The identity you encounter
Rising out from the murky deep

We cried.

At the end of the period as the class was leaving, Abe pulled Lexie off to the side to thank her. She had seen that he was going down but had kept her cool and given Abe the help he needed.

Lexie leaned on his desk and looked him square in the eyes firing back a point-blank range, "I'm a lifeguard, Mr. Abe." Then taking a short breath, shaking her head just as she had done twenty-four hours earlier, added her stinger, "And you are stubborn." I think that was the nicest compliment any one has ever given me, for in my weakness, Lexie had seen the strength of my unwavering choice to carry on.

The rusty nut had finally loosened as my illusion of control had disappeared, and I would become secure with my students. From that day on, every morning from across the room, Lexie would turn her face towards me and ask, "How are you today, Mr. Abe?" She watched me, and would not look away, waiting for me to answer with my eyes, and then would know it was safe for her, the school, and Abe to all carry on. Humbled by my students—forever my teacher, they will be.

CHAPTER 9

Bald is Beautiful— A Mirror Reflection

At 30 years old I was fearful of rejection, and mind games annoyed me, having zero patience for trying to guess what a girlfriend may be thinking. So, I was never much for dating, and was a loner who had just departed from moldy money to buy my own house…to the delight of my parents, who hoped this might turn into something bigger.

I met Kris at a dance. Though I was not looking for anyone, from a distance I saw her. When our eyes met, keeping my cowboy hat on I nodded, pointing to the dance floor—then Kris turned to look behind her as if expecting to find somebody else waving back at me, but no, she was the one I wanted.

We kicked up our heels for a while, then the music slowed. I had never felt this way before, comfortable. The moment I put my hands on her waist I smiled and Kris asked, "Do you always smile like this?"

"I love life." There was a twinkle in my eyes.

"A man after my own heart," Kris responded. She didn't know how close to the truth that was because for me it was love at first sight and I knew I would be marrying her. But I thought I'd better ask for her phone number first. We said good night and I drove back to my new home alone.

The next morning, after meeting my wife-to-be, I called Dad and told him he didn't need the "Wife Wanted" sign he jokingly had threatened to put above my garage door. But three weeks would pass before I would call Kris, and it wasn't because I had forgotten or lost her number—I had been consumed by the process of moving into my new home, and building a nest takes time. Being sequential, I moved like a turtle. Finally, with things in order, I was ready. Ready, that is, to take a well-planned trip up to the Boundary Waters Canoe Area. After getting back, the fuchsia baskets were bone dry and needed immediate watering. I then took the napkin that had Kris's phone number on it out of my wallet. Destiny, this was one of the few times that I would not fret over needing control. I would just let it happen.

"Hello," Kris answered the phone. I told her that this was Dan and to my surprise she asked, "Who?" Taking me back, I had to remind her that I wore a cowboy hat when we danced the night away. Then she told me where to go, giving me directions, that is.

I went to pick her up without wearing a hat. Losing my hair shortly after high school, the little hair I had remaining around the back and sides was shaved off. This would be our first official date.

Rapping on the farmhouse door made the flies jump off the screen. Kris opened it to greet me and the first thing that came out of her mouth was, "You didn't tell me you didn't have any hair."

Oh, Kris was a good one. She had an eye for beauty and spoke straight forwardly, saying what was on her mind. My shoulder blades went back, almost touching each other, and with chest held high blurted out a grateful praise, "Thanks!"

Kris had complimented me on my best phenotype. The brain would believe anything you tell it, but you have to say it out loud. Abe would soon use this mindset to show his students the power of spoken word.

●●●

In Abe's classroom there hung a concave mirror. As his students got closer and closer, it would increasingly magnify every part of their reflection. Before class started students viewed it from a distance and then anxious as to what it might reveal would sneak up to the mirror to take a peek at themselves—a pimple or blemish, the smallest imperfection could not hide from it, causing students to back off and quickly move away. But Abe would never run from the mirror.

It was the very first day of the semester and Abe introduced himself, as he always had, by boldly standing in front of the mirror with his face filling the frame. He crowed, "Bald is Beautiful...Bald is Beautiful...Bald is Beautiful!" Through the enchantment of these three words Abe hoped his students would accept and think differently about any perceived unbecoming attributes that they perhaps were unable to change in themselves. Adding to this hope, Abe also thought—albeit, maybe for only just a moment, this might minimize a problem they now carried. After all, what could be a scarier projection for a high schooler than for them to think they could lose all their hair?

Students inscribed those very words: "Bald is Beautiful!" on the poster paper surrounding the edges of the mirror. The three-worded phrase was praise with a permeating message that had become legendary even to students that didn't have Abe as a teacher. For all things were beautiful—and Abe in his own mind, and in theirs, was legend. There had been times when teaching was magic, until a spell would sometimes come upon him and try to take it away.

•••

The middle school teachers warned the high school staff about the incoming freshmen, who had branded themselves with unprecedented, infamous notoriety. This entire eighth grade class had been kicked out of the Science Museum of Minnesota and been banned from coming back—forever!

Well, Abe couldn't ban them from his classroom so in they came, marching into his last period when he was most sorely lacking of energy. And it was true—they were bullies and misfits; every one of them was an unopened can of soup, ready to explode. Some literally hiding under their desks while Abe tried to take attendance, while another student lay on top of the counter with his head under a laboratory faucet trying to drink water. The static of negative vibes quickly exceeded capacity, pushing all sanity out of the room, and blinding Abe from any good that possibly could have been in there. They were a handful of thorns with no flowers, buds, or a single petal in sight.

Lessons learned, even for a teacher, need confirmation. All it took was for Abe to be gone from his classroom for a day. Upon his return the next day, Abe looked down on his desk at what may as well have been his epitaph. Written with a red wax marking pen in Abe's lesson plan book with print so large it covered Monday thru Friday was this message: "Dear Mr. Abrahamson, I feel so bad for you. It is not your fault, but please don't call me back. I will never substitute teach this class again!!!"

Abe was losing his magic and started hating the very students he should love. They held all the power, and he wondered how long their cruel tricks would keep him in their spell.

Ryan's long greasy hair came down to his shoulders and had been dyed jet-black to match his painted fingernails. He sat next to a girl, who like him, wore Goth-like attire, but whose face was so finely decorated by a cosmetic covering she could have been on the front page of a glamour magazine. Abe chose not believe the rumors that she had been caught in school last year doing tricks to eighth grade boys for lunch money. He felt pain with the memory and loss of his former student Katie, whose classmates had labeled her a "whore" and he knew how quickly rumors can inflict harm—even in thought, Abe could not lose another student.

It was already two weeks into the quarter and Abe hadn't yet talked with Ryan or his friends and was purposefully avoiding them. Their seats had been assigned to the back row. Class was about to begin, and as he was taking attendance Abe found himself walking past Ryan's desk in the back of the room. Then Ryan lifted his long stringy hair away from his eyes and looked up pointing to Abe—his finger curled, motioning for Abe to come closer. A heavy cloud of perfume from Ryan's neighbor surrounded him and, in a whisper,, he spoke, "You know, Mr. Abe if it wasn't for this class, I wouldn't have anything to look forward to."

Abe paused, disarmed, and in an apologetic tone he uttered, "Thank you." He should have known better than to judge a book by its cover. Ryan's words, spoken softly, cut Abe to the quick proving his own hidden prejudice so wrong and at the same time, through this compliment, lifted Abe to the highest level. Ryan had put to practice what Danny had discovered long ago—Gracious Inclusion. But instead of coming from Abe, it now came from a student. It was times like these when Abe became so small and then smaller yet that others became infinitely large—far beyond his comprehension. All was one as Ryan won Abe over taking him to the other side. As the cliché goes, a child shall lead them. And the equation of "Win-One" ($n/1 \times 1/n = 1$) showed. Unity in reciprocity—once again independently proven and so unexpectedly tested through time. That's how I know this to be true: Gracious Inclusion works for others, too.

Words are powerful, especially when they come unsolicited from a student. Empowered students show their faces. Abe spent time getting to know Ryan and his friends. He jokingly told them, "You can't help it having all that hair."

"Ya, we know," they laughed. "Because bald is beautiful."

The next day Abe's sour class of ninth graders were at their worst, draining his gas tank and filling it with negative electricity that was useless to a carburetor that had coughed its last breath. Past baggage had been carried for a long time and Abe recognized the masks of disguised expressions that covered his students' faces. Then he was prompted to join them—a playful force which changed the polarity placed Abe in a new vehicle that moved him. He flippantly said to them, "You are my favorite class!" Hybrids run fast on electricity and news travels fast through a grapevine of teenagers.

The following morning first hour class came in and asked Abe why last hour was his favorite. Words had taken them down to their worst and now words would take them up to their best. And they did become his favorite class. Rhubarb sure tastes good with sugar—as the magic had returned.

For so long Abe's seating charts were filled with smiley faces, frowns, and questions marks written out in faint pencil lines next to names of the good, the bad, and the ones that potentially could be a problem. Students who struggled often received comments on their report cards sent home: "Negative Attitude" or "Disrespectful." These words cut into their character. But now, those pencil marks on Abe's seating chart had been erased. Abe had finally begun to change the antecedent of his expectations and his own attitude. With a twist in his thinking,

Gracious Inclusion would work as he began to put "Positive Attitude" on all their report cards. Knowing it not to be a lie, but true—even though it was not where some students were at, it was a wish for where Abe knew they could be. If student grades were due to low test scores or not handing in work, it was also noted with the subjective comment of "positive attitude" always tagged with these objective comments. The result was changed behavior. Kids will live up to how they are labeled despite their appearance at the time.

By quarter's end, Ryan was selected as Abe's student of the quarter. As Abe presented Ryan with his certificate award, Ryan once again pushed his hair away from his eyes and looked straight into Abe's and said, "The best grade I ever got in science before was a 'D.'" Ryan smiled for he had proudly earned an "A-."

I am grateful for what Ryan taught me about myself, our class and "book covers." You give what you have received, and we had lifted each other to the nth degree—a lesson in giving.

Looking in the mirror I could say "Bald is Beautiful," but by looking into the eyes of my students I could see beauty beyond a mask of makeup or any darkened facade. And so, a bald-headed teacher and a group of misfits led by a greasy, long-haired student celebrated not only differences but the freedom to express ourselves, revealing the true character that lay deep within. And with it came laughter.

CHAPTER 10

Honey, I'm Home—Money Woes

It was a week before winter break and in the dark school parking lot Abe cried as he looked at the 100 Grand candy bar that had been given to him by a school board member before the start of a short and fruitless negotiation. Words that were spoken just fifteen minutes before echoed in his mind "Don't spend it all in one spot, and Merry Christmas." Those words spoken in jest, cut into him. Integrity is what you do when no one else is watching. Like roof trusses hidden in the attic, they do their job holding the heavy weight of snow from unyielding blizzards, but this storm was too heavy and Abe was breaking. He was alone and swallowing his pride he ate the candy bar. The staff had taught for two years without a settled contract and negotiations were at a standstill.

This was not the game of Monopoly, which he so often played as Danny with his siblings, but one that tested the real strength of his own adult integrity. Abe felt defeated. As a child he had experienced losing, and he once again brushed the tears away. With money being tight, he was led to reflect on his own commitments—not only to being a teacher but supporting his family. Knowing there were so many jobs that are higher paying out there, he started to question the choice of his profession. But when you start comparing, you bet against your dream.

Abe was young and in the first few years of his teaching. Kris was a stay-at-home mom and with their first children being twins, they struggled to make ends meet.

Coming home from work that night Abe opened the door from the garage. Out from the sky a diaper dropped, plopping down at his feet. *Chutes Away,* he thought—but this was not a board game that delivered relief to the accident site. Instead it brought the accident site to Abe, the relief. He started counting the number of diapers that had been tossed down the stairway that day. And with twins that were teething, Abe needed more than his ten fingers to add them up. No need ask how Kris's day had gone...counting gave him the answer.

Abe trudged up the fourteen steps and opened the gate at the top. Life was good—even as another unserviced load came crawling to greet him. Abe pinched his nose saying, "Here comes the baby with pants full of gravy." Thoughts about using cloth diapers to save money had been there, but with rinsing them in the toilet, soaking them in Dreft, then laundering—no way. On the counter, bottles had been washed and sterilized, and Abe knew by the volume of milk that had been expressed, and supplemented baby formula, it would be his turn for midnight feedings.

In the morning at school, Abe's students gauged the kind of night he had had—again, there was no need for inquiry—

with his droopy eyes and the stubble on his face, they knew. He looked at his calculations that had been scribbled on the U.S. Army military desk pad calendar the recruiters always gave the school. Abe counted the ways to save and even anticipated the net gain switching from baby formula to whole milk. Once any new contract was settled, Abe could figure to the penny what his new monthly check would clear.

Over the years the twins grew out of diapers and two more children would come. Four total—all within a five-year period. When at school, Abe's students would continue to check on him, as he would check on them. But now in mid-life crisis, he looked down at his desk calendar, empty of any figuring and scribbled calculations, for another long and grueling teacher contract negotiation was going nowhere.

●●●

I did not want to feel forced to leave my dream. During stressful times, I often sort out my feelings through an expression of poetry. While contemplating whether I, as Abe, could or even should stay in teaching, out came a poem that I gave copies of to my fellow colleagues:

A Calling

When I became a teacher
I never thought about making plenty of "dough."
I truly believed that "enough was enough,"
for all I wanted was the "cake"
while others planned for "icing" piled high.
Was my choice a big mistake?

Honey, I'm Home—Money Woes

It's hard to stay an idealist and care for life's progeny...
Many times, my resolve has been tested,

I struggle to remain free.
But freedom means to have an option, monetarily.

For you see the "cake" I held had to be eaten,
Look...there has never been any extra on the shelf.
With cupboards bare, my thoughts turn to family and self.

As you, too, look inward what do you find
in the mind, will, and emotion of your soul?
Does turmoil drive you to protectively act,
through pride and self-control?

Philosophy transferred to life's real situations,
is what it appears to be.
I believe that kids are worth it,
I will fight to protect my identity.
I hope this is true for all teachers, new and old.
For today we are called with this message,
to stand tall and unashamedly bold.

(Staff, thank you for being a teacher, 2:30 A.M. to bed I
must go. Tired, but with clear resolve.)

Sincerely,
Dan Abrahamson

When you lose in Monopoly, you want to play again. And with his metal being tested years before, Abe had not let the angry red markings from a substitute teacher who vowed never to return to his classroom ruin the lesson plans of his life, nor would any unsettled contract do the same.

Abe was a teacher.

CHAPTER 11

Clear the Clutter to Find the Kid...It was Time

Behavior problems for too many was the norm as Abe's students continued to believe they were failures. A belief reinforced by returning crimson-covered tests to them, slashed for all to see. For twenty years of teaching against a standard, he had used a benchmark that was rigid, and like a metal measuring tape, inflexible. With a sense of justice and fair play, Abe had set kids up to compete against each other, with their grades posted in the hallway like a scoreboard that read: "Home Team—PASSING, Visiting Posts—UTTER FAILURES." But Abe, too, felt like a failure. With so much clutter between him and those failures, his measuring tape was rendered useless.

Failures forgot to bring pencils and notebooks to class. Failures didn't listen. Failures were tardy. Failures became disconnected and were not part of the class. Failures were Posts who walked past Abe in the hallway and did not look him in the eyes for they had no eyes for which to see, nor ears to hear.

•••

Several years had passed since Brad had silently dropped out of school and disappeared. It was summertime, and my twins were only knee high to a grasshopper at the time. We were out to get some groceries when Brad stumbled out of the adjoining liquor store and glaringly looked up at me. With a loosened tongue, he spewed, "Ha, Abrahamson..." and then snarling through his blackened teeth he spat, "Get out of my fuckin' life!" The Post now had a voice. One of which, I would have struck out against if not with my children, but instead I whisked them away. His explosive words rocked me backwards, stirring up entangled memories as if it were yesterday.

Five years of failure. Five years of offering to help Brad—who showed no response, only muted indifference. I thought I had done all that I could for him, but he was a "Post" and refused to change. Now, carrying a paper bag in his hand, we had stood on the sidewalk.

My frustration morphed into anger, for it was no longer teacher to student. Brad had crossed the line and trespassed into my private world, hissing his toxic venom not only on me but also my children. In so many cases I had felt the welder's torch cut as well as mend, but with Brad the heat had not cooled, wounds remained open. It was a messy and complicated intersection. Judgement is exclusionary and had now become a two-way street with ill-feelings crashing from both directions.

Brad had branded me with his own letter "F" and like Todd smacking me over the head with my Zorro lunch box, had also stolen control. But neither Danny back then nor would I now succumb to the notion that a dent would make a lunch box or a life a piece of junk. These feelings of unresolved conflict would be my beast of burden.

•••

Ten years later Brad's stormy confrontation was still brewing inside of Abe, fermenting. The growing evidence of a failing teaching method had snowballed into a movement that demanded truth to be found in proof. As a science teacher, Abe was not a stranger to collecting data to substantiate claims, but he still remained blind as to how Gracious Inclusion could be put into the classroom. Before him sat the Genetics tests his class had just finished. Years of frustration had taught Abe the defensive practice called the "art of separation," where the cream rises to the top. *I'll first correct Teresa's,* he thought. *She's such a bright girl.* And sure enough, just as expected, Teresa aced it. Abe quickly recorded 100% on the top of her test, put a smiley face by her name and wrote, "Way to go!" The next twenty students earned grades far above the 60% pass/fail cut off. With these scores, Abe patted himself on the back. He smiled, satisfied—knowing he had done his job.

Purposely set aside, like so many times before, was the other stack of tests. Abe was not so quick to look at these because he knew they would try to ruin his day. None of these test scores would even reach the 50th percentile because they were from Posts. One Post, just days before had come back from a two-week vacation, not taken during spring break, but rather when their time-share slot was available. Upon return the student asked, "Mr. Abe, did I miss anything?"

Sarcasm pushed against this perceived insincerity. "No," Abe responded. "We waited for you." He then suggested some time slots for making up the work.

"I think I'll be just fine," the Post shrugged, "I'll just take the test." Other Posts had been physically present but checked out as if on vacation, their minds somewhere else other than school.

Posts had their grip on Abe and he had his grip on them in an interlocking quandary. Abe's hope was in the trash basket and not expecting anything different, he clutched his pen so hard his knuckles became white. Reluctantly he began correcting their tests and soon with a deep sigh, he whispered under his breath a conditioned response, "Stupid is as stupid does." Their tests bled red, covering their pages, making him feel powerless, disconnected and icky inside. This was the same icky feeling that had come back to visit, just as it had hounded him all the way up to this point in his teaching career. The tighter Abe held on the worse it became, and they were pulling him under. Mystifying it was, to watch his dream of making a difference to everyone slowly die. He was drowning with them and would have to let go to come up for air.

Abe stared at the rusted footings of his file cabinets which were filled with relics that he had never been able to discard even though they took up valuable space: hundreds of manila folders holding tests, worksheets, and documents once so important. But now the blue mimeographed information, having faded long after the alcohol had evaporated off the printed page, was unreadable. There they remained—entombed. Then Abe returned to the conundrum before him.

Pushing the tests away, Abe squeezed his eyes tight, shutting out the light and thought of Brad. In his heart, he started to believe Brad did care and had wanted to tell him his life was FUBAR. His snarling admission was not directed to be offensive to Abe but aimed back at himself. Perhaps, it wasn't that Brad was refusing to change, but rather was not able.

If Brad was not able to change, who would? Abe had found himself a slave to the very tool created to serve him, his measuring tape—the test, used as a benchmark to measure students' successes and failures against the standard, separated Abe from the ones he could not reach. He had lost so many battles. This wasn't the way it was supposed to be.

Abe would reflect on where his attitude had put his students and what it had done to him. The practice of being kind through inclusion had become addictive, and proven time after time, it would grow. Smiling, Abe had seen his circle expand, but what about all the Posts in his classroom? How could he find smiles for all of them? What he was doing was not working, and so it must have been wrong—moving against the power of inclusion.

Abe was no longer blind, but still sorely bound by conventional prejudices and guidelines. The waves of repeated failures sought to crumble the rock of past practices. Abe would surrender to their force and join them on the sandy shore—he was once again being broken. For mountains make pebbles, and pebbles make mountains. In reciprocity he would become small making them large.

The waves had done their work moving Abe in a different direction, not away from the slackers, shakers and vacation takers, but toward them. He put his red pen down and cried out, "I can't do this any longer!"

For it was Abe, not his students, who had failed. It was time to rectify an injustice to which he, for years, had been an accomplice. Letting go, Abe would no longer try to hang on to this illusion of control. Abe had something that Danny had carried with him all along—a predisposition to protect the vulnerable. Like Danny in the third grade looking at Benny laying on the cold cement floor, Abe knew what had to be done—graciousness is inclusive.

Abe would connect to those who were lost by doing something unprecedented. In defiance of past practice, it would no longer be his job to fail kids or hold them up to a benchmark that would label them as losers. Instead it became his job to reach them—all of them.

It was time to clear the clutter, not to find the measuring tape, but to find the kid. Instead of putting a big red "F" on the top of their papers, in green ink Abe wrote, "Please, see me." And with that note he placed a smiley face by each of their names. For the first time in his life, as a teacher, no matter what the score, Abe smiled correcting all of the tests, and could not wait to give them back to his students.

The next day tests were handed back. Posts began talking with other Posts showing each other what had been written on top of their test papers. Soldiers in the military know their position or rank, and so it is with students. The rank of Posts stirred. Something was happening to the outcast of bottom dwellers. One Post came up to Abe with a confused look, pointing to what he had written on his test, "Hey, Mr. A, what's this all about?"

Abe looked into Charlie's eyes and gave him a summons, "3:15, after school, see me. You'll be OK." Smiling, Abe now had a plan.

It was now 3:15 and Charlie's six foot-three-inch, 400-pound body stood, filling the entrance to the classroom door. "Well, come on in," Abe beckoned.

"I don't know if I can." Charlie stood motionless, "I mean I don't know how." Charlie had made himself look small.

The unknown was threatening and to step into waters always thought to be too deep required one thing—trust. Abe had seen the face of fear so many times in the past. It showed on Charlie's face. "Just take one step and you're in. Everything will be alright."

With that, Charlie blew apprehension out of bellowing cheeks and said, "OK" and took his first step into becoming part of the class.

Abe pulled out Charlie's test and in disbelief shook his head, "You had a tough time with this Genetics test. You know this stuff better than that don't you?"

Charlie nodded and faintly uttered, "Ya, I guess so."

They sat down at a table together and Charlie leaned way back in his chair, crossing his arms like a frozen snowman. A distant gaze from eyes of coal showed Charlie had put himself on a familiar pathway, transporting himself far, far away. "Knock, knock," Abe's knuckles wrapped on the table. "Charlie, I know you're in there."

Then, as if being awakened too early from a nap, Charlie came out of the fog and snapped back, announcing, "You know I didn't bring a pencil."

Charlie never brought a pencil to class. His head flopped down on the table, assuming his usual helpless position. "You never bring a pencil," Abe chuckled, "but that's OK because we don't have any paper."

Pushing the old test to the side, Abe opened the textbook to the first page of the Genetics chapter and pointed to the picture of a mother deer nursing her fawn. "Charlie, tell me about this picture."

"Well," Charlie said softly. "The phenotype of the mom deer is albino. That's because she has two small a's in her genotype."

Abe's mouth fell wide open and blurted, "Wow!"

"Didn't I say it right?" Charlie asked with a worried look. "No, I mean...yes. It was more than right. You're an Einstein!"

Charlie's eyes watered and he looked at Abe as if being awakened from believing in a lie. "You mean I'm not stupid?"

Charlie started to shine and continued his dissertation. "I know that the fawn's father, even though not in the picture, must not be albino. Because the male gamete must have carried a big 'A' to fertilize the small 'a' egg from the mom to produce this offspring, which is heterozygous 'Aa.' If I had a damn...oops, I mean, darn pencil, I could show you with one of those four squares the odds of this happening."

Charlie then turned the page for himself. "There," he said, pointing to the Punnett square diagram in the textbook. "See, just like I told ya."

More genetics terms and concepts flowed out of Charlie as he connected with each picture. Abe then smiled, and said three little words, "You are passing."

Abe glanced at his closed file cabinets which were filled with faded relics representing his past practice. Then he pointed to Charlie's failed exam, setting up an agreement, "From now on, anytime you don't pass a test like this, stop in and show me what you know. You'll be fine." Charlie looked at Abe and gave him a smile that sealed the pact between them. They now had something that before was missing—an essential ingredient, called trust. There are no stupid kids, just stupid or wrong assessments.

Instead of using another same old paper and pencil test as a measuring tape, Abe had reached out and given Charlie an empty jar. Charlie filled that jar to overflowing with what was inside of him. It blew beyond Abe's expectations. The jar was made of clear glass and they could see all that had been put in it. The connections Charlie had made for himself were meaningful and of value. He was proud of what he had done. Waters would never again be too deep, for Charlie now knew how to swim.

It would not be easy, but I knew this to be true—we are not alone, nor ever would we be. The next day Charlie was the first one to class and in his heart, he carried a new expectation—hope. For in his hand, he held a pencil.

"Guess what," he told his friends. "I'm passing!" Smiling, they sat down, and Charlie told them more. He had filled a jar and was now part of the class. Charlie was using his voice. He had a true sense of self-worth and was now spreading it to others. Having hope is not enough. It must be connected to trust and put into action.

Later in the week, Abe saw Charlie walking down the hallway. Abe raised his hand for a high five as they approached each other. Charlie raised his big hand and slapped it into Abe's with a loud smack. Abe continued to walk, but his hand stayed, for Charlie's grip had wrapped around Abe's and did not let go. Stretching his arm like a rubber band Charlie pulled Abe back and looked straight into his eyes, giving him his best, "Have a good day, Mr. Abe."

When you find something good, you don't want to let go.

CHAPTER 12

Inclusion—Something Inside Demands It

Danny looked down at his half dissected fetal pig that lay on the wax pan. Biology period for his lab work never seemed to have enough time and today Danny felt compelled to take part of the dismembered oinker home. It was the head that had proven to be the most delicate and demanding area of dissection, and so, leaving the body with umbilical cord still attached behind, he plopped just the head into his empty sandwich bag and took it home.

After supper, with operating tools in hand, a scalpel from school and a hack-saw from his dad's workshop, Danny diligently worked at removing the skull. Finally finishing the task while watching Johnny Carson, the brain was free for further exploration. The Amygdala, found in all mammals, was between the two temporal lobes, superior to the brainstem. Danny thought it funny to think that he too had one.

Whether sad, happy, angry or afraid the face gives voice to a personified amygdala, which I now call Amy-G-Dala. Emotions could close or open the gateway into the inner workings of the classroom. Danny's days when he was much younger would also continue to be a connector.

Danny had always been a hands-on learner. Even as a toddler, he knew square, round, and triangular pegs all had to fit into square, round, and triangular holes. Once they fit, a wooden hammer was used to tap them through to the other side and then Danny tipped the peg board upside down—tapping and pounding resumed. This is when I learned a lesson that would find conflict within it…things fit where they were made to belong, and square pegs don't fit into round holes.

It was an easy transfer for me to see classrooms were like peg boards. As a teacher, Abe used a wooden hammer to pound information into his class with lab activities, experiments, and practice problems, trying to prove they are all made to fit. Day after day, Abe flipped the peg board over and did the same thing all over again, but sometimes kids didn't fit and raw emotions flowed out from the amygdala onto their faces, including his own.

●●●

It was near the end of the quarter and Suzie, a Special Education Para, walked into Abe's room waving an I.E.P., delivering the unavoidably anticipated news, "Mr. Abrahamson, a new student will be joining your Biology class next quarter." Abe's face contorted. Suzie couldn't leave soon enough and now during his teacher prep, Abe, the biologist, scraped off a fresh culture of cells from the nutrient agar. Placing them on the slide, he peered into the microscope, opening up a whole new big world that performed on the stage below.

As the cells danced, Abe was intrigued by their importance and they appeared so very large to him. He seemed to hear them boast, "See how we move...all things alive must be made of us." Stellar—like the Big Bang—their importance seemed to expand beyond the observable boundaries of the cosmos. But then Abe, the chemist, began thinking...*Smaller is not lesser in importance.* And in this conversion of thought there would be no notion of one-upmanship, but instead a connection of interdependencies that often were hidden.

Abe, the Biologist and Chemist, was compelled to find the connection between his two worlds. Being a teacher, he wondered how Suzie and the I.E.P. would fit in. Abe looked at the I.E.P. that had been forced upon him, and then he refocused on the cells that needed a microscope to be seen, but in importance to life had appeared so very large to him. Watching the cells, he thought nothing could be too small to be insignificant.

Cells are essential to life, but they must follow suit like everything else by relying on something smaller than themselves in order to survive. Our cells need three molecules: Glucose, Water, and Oxygen. If cells starve, dehydrate, or suffocate they will die.

Looking up at the periodic table, Abe knew so much could be hiding—like burning sugar reveals carbon as a backbone and passing electricity through water separates the breathable oxygen from the explosive hydrogen hidden therein. The identifiable properties of all elements within molecules wait to be discovered through change.

And now, as Abe walked down the hallway, Suzie motioned for him to come into the SpEd Room. There sat Margret, wearing a glum look on her face. Pulling another desk next to hers, he sat down and started to introduce himself. "I'm Mr. Abra...."

Margret interrupted, "You're Mr. Abrahamson," she said, almost breaking a smiling. "I got you next quarter." She looked down at a Biology worksheet that had no questions answered.

"So," Abe observed, looking at the empty page, "you don't have anything written down here."

Margret slumped down in her desk and mumbled out of the side of her mouth, "This stuff is stupid, and Suzie's crabby. She won't help me with it."

"Let me tell you a story about a little boy named Tommy. He wants to build a dog house." Margret's foot started tapping and as if reading music off a written page Abe connected the story to protein synthesis.

Margret then rose from her desk and walked over to Suzie. "Hey, Suzie, have I got a story to tell you." Margret shared it, word for word with Suzie. They both smiled and for good reason.

The amygdala is tied to the emotional memory center directing stress management. And Amy-G-Dala, known to have a reputation of being quite temperamental in all of us at critical times, rules. Making demands beyond those of ordinary cells—in addition to glucose, water, and oxygen, Amy has two other requirements: safety and human connection. Take security away or put someone in isolation and in time these cells will also die. The two are intertwined; from safety, relationships flourish, and out of relationships, security is assured. Take harmful stress away and let the learning begin.

The following day, Margret came up to Abe in the hallway. Inside a circle she had drawn pictures of the story about Tommy building his doghouse with the title, "The Cell Made Easy." Margret loved to draw and shared her gift and that's how she understood.

Square pegs can't be forced into small round holes. It is common practice to make a new class for the pegs that don't fit in, but I have found that this is not "best practice," for the minute you tailor a class for square pegs, a triangle-shaped peg soon comes around the corner.

Abe found ways to be graciously inclusive—by making the round hole larger, no matter what their shape, all the square and triangle pegs can fit in and be part of something bigger than themselves. Knowing Abe wallpapered poems and posters all over his classroom, a student gave him one of their own to display:

Knowing Yourself

I fit into this world where I do, and when I don't,
I move to where I do fit,
because I won't change myself to fit somewhere I don't.

Kids give the best unfiltered insight because aging can cloud the eyes. Abe taped the poem behind the glass of one of his cabinet doors for all to see. Like a loom, each thread had been tightly woven into the fabric called a class. Protecting the ties that bind would prove to be an ongoing challenge.

•••

All of Abe's students were to take a State-mandated Biology test. Every student would have the test read to them through head phones as they sat in front of a computer screen, which visually displayed each question. However, due to their I.E.P.'s, he was told the Special Ed students in his class would not be going down with the rest of the class to take the test in the Media Center. When the Special Ed students caught wind of this—with their equilibria rocking— they sailed into the classroom demanding an answer and wanting normalcy. They baulked, "Hey Mr. A, why can't we go with everyone else?"

An uninvited and unwanted cold feeling of alienation came upon them and temperaments would flare up. Abe knew all too well the fear that being separated could instill and where there's smoke there would still be fire. His kindled brain did not have far to travel. The fabric of interconnected dependencies that insured safety was about to be cut and it teetered in jeopardy. For all threads were needed and tightly woven, not one could be lost. Deep within, Amy-G-Dala screamed, "Stop, no more."

"I'm sorry," Abe apologized. "Your names are just on the list. And your I.E.P.'s say you must have the test read to you." Constraints dictate—and they were locked into standardized frameworks, which bullied not only his students, but also Abe as a teacher. Labels exclude, alienate, chop and dice until no former sense of self-recognition remains. Mending connections takes longer than breaking them and messing with the emotions of Abe's students had tapped into a backlog of accruing debt. A debt that students held against a heartless institution. Over time, waiting could only give pause to further questioning of a weakening line of credit. This event was filled with emptiness—nonsense, because Abe knew the test would be read to all students. He brought this to the attention of the Special Ed department, but nothing changed.

Two days later, these students were once again separated from the class to take the same test wearing the same headphones with no teacher reading the test to them. There was no need to be separated. While they were taking their tests the other students and Abe would be forced to start a new unit without them and a needless hole had grown larger. Loosened threads lay disconnected from the rest.

Lies bully, taking freedom by telling you how you do or don't fit in, and what achievement looks like. Labels, meant to act as shields, are actually sharp, white-hot daggers, cauterizing as they cut—keeping the blood from being shed. So, failing to see the bloodshed, the system is preserved and it continues. Labels imprinted at critical times are not easily, or perhaps for that matter, ever erased. All-the-while the Amygdala slowly dies, disturbed by separation. This was hard for me to swallow. However, it was on my plate.

Human relationships and security, so often hidden, will never be directly observed through a microscope or on the periodic table hanging on a wall. But herein lies the quest.

To the Biologist, cells are in a dynamic ongoing flux of homeostasis, and to the Chemist, disturbed reactions are destined to seek equilibrium. To lose one is to lose the other: for life, connected by a spark to a handful of chemicals, will always have stressors to be found and felt by the teacher and student alike in a test tube called the classroom.

And Abe would continue to comfort the disturbed and disturb the comfortable.

CHAPTER 13

Gracious Inclusion...
Just Hall Duty?

Like the invisible force of gravity, Gracious Inclusion has always waited to be discovered, but all too often remains hidden by a mask of fear. Teetering at the precipice of change during critical times in my life I, as Abe, the teacher, or Danny, the child, had felt its nudge. Asking me to let go and trust, Gracious Inclusion waited to be put into practice where I would again experience the exhilaration of free-falling into its safe embrace.

Stored in a cubby-hole next to the science office was a student desk that had the word "F-u-c-k" anonymously carved into it making it an outcast, no longer of value, ruined and of little use. But it was time for hall duty and being the only desk available, Abe would have to sit in it.

How can I use it? Abe thought. *A teacher should not sit in front of such obscenity.* So, Abe covered the indelible mark with masking tape making the desk ready to be recommissioned.

The sound of footsteps awakened Abe to a presence that was about to come around the corner. Looking up, a student walked toward him. Sometimes students would avoid making eye contact with Abe as they walked by, looking at the walls, floor or ceiling, but Abe always searched, hoping to connect. Abe didn't need to know the person—to him no one was a stranger, but everyone was a little strange. This student chose not to look away and looked into Abe's eyes confirming an awareness of each other.

Then as if hitting a tiny speed bump in the road the student's head slightly tilted back with a nod so subtle that it would have been missed if not for eyes, not bouncing, but tied to the other's in a straight line. Abe returned the acknowledgement by slightly raising his index finger, which like a windshield wiper quickly swept the events of the moment from right to left, stopping as it pointed to the student.

Smiles of acceptance were simultaneously exchanged as they passed each other, and then Abe made an about-face, turning as if he had forgotten something and with a few skips caught up to the student. Now going in the same direction, Abe held the science pod door open, letting the student enter first, and with a second door to open, the student reciprocated the accommodation by doing the same for Abe. The student disappeared around the corner into a classroom. *What a nice kid,* Abe thought.

As that thought still lingered, an unwanted seed of suspicion was about to be planted, challenging the warm feeling of inclusion. Abe went to retrieve the desk from the nearby storage area and he saw the tape had been torn off.

The obscenity flashed like a neon sign and was shouting at him. More tape was used, but it was always removed the next day. Abe tried scribbling over the four letters, but the deep grooves of defacement were not able to be covered, hidden, or blotted out. It could not be silenced.

Something else was going on here and as more days passed Abe tired. It was only then, resigning from his futile efforts, Abe seemed to hear a knock as if coming from the other side of a locked door. Maybe the desktop was really an ongoing journal, one in which he was supposed to open and add to. So, underneath the vulgarity, Abe wrote his own 4 lettered word—it read "L-o-v-e."

The next morning "L-o-v-e" had not been erased. The ghost-writer, whose hand time and time again had given voice to the desktop, really wanted to be found and had "knocked on the door" for one last time by writing: "What is Love?" It was now time for Abe to search and travel on a pathway.

Later at home that night, Abe tried to juggle his thoughts—muddled they had become. Then, as if awakened from a deep sleep, science would be used to answer the ghost-writer's question. Water can look differently as a gas, liquid, or solid, but don't be fooled, they are all made of the same molecules. Abe had failed to observe what was before his very eyes—we are all different and yet the same. This is to know "L-o-v-e." It is all encompassing.

The next day, as Abe found hall duty was over, he pushed the desk that he had been sitting on towards the storage area. A student saw him, smiled, and asked, "Can I help you with that desk?" Abe looked down at the desktop and couldn't help but wonder if this student knew more than he let on and then the student opened the door for him. To all the ghost-writers out there keep writing, the circle expands.

"The Circle of Gracious Inclusion"

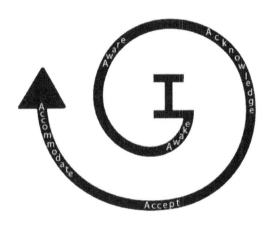

We are not always aware of putting Gracious Inclusion to practice. In retrospect I look back and realize it was always at work, for the Five A's of Gracious Inclusion were breadcrumbs that had unknowingly dropped out of a back pocket along a path that marks where, when, and how inclusion happened: Awake and Aware, Acknowledge, Accept, Accommodate now with no regrets.

The Five A's of Gracious Inclusion were all there. Both Danny and Abe had seen the power of the Five A's working together and the consequences when they had been separated. One leads to the next, providing a way to think beyond oneself—Gracious Inclusion expands. Now, during hall duty Abe had and would continue to experience its power once again.

Most communication in the school corridors does not take place through a desktop and the best advice given to Abe by a principal was, "When on hall duty, look at their faces." This advice always stayed with him, for the face does not lie, nor can it hide.

Some hall duties are quiet like a calm ocean, while others are full of non-stop waves following one after another. Today, Abe would be caught up in the rhythm of the wave's cadence. Some waves are bigger than others and Abe would not know how big this one was until it came splashing into his own classroom.

Kyle was a student from Abe's first semester of Biology and when he realized he would not have Abe for the second half he was very disturbed—he came into the classroom teary-eyed. Abe's Biology class was over its limit, but he knew that he could not lose Kyle and so he went down to the counseling office. Abe had made room for him.

And now while on hall duty, Kyle cruised past Abe down the hallway. "Kyle," he summoned. Kyle stopped and turned around, lumbering back to him. "You're the man!" Abe said.

"I know I am, Mr. A." Kyle grinned and with tightened fists, their knuckles crashed together in a routine that now was customarily expected, and yet, always enjoyed as if it were the first encounter. Kyle then headed back to class.

As a teacher you don't always know why you connect with certain students, but long after having Kyle as a student I would find out that my rapport with Kyle was more important to him than I could have ever known. I learned about an atrocity inflicted upon Kyle as a child.

Knowledge is enlightening—I was told Kyle was a bed-wetter. At home, after wetting the bed he was told he was "filthy" and then sprayed down with the garden hose and forced to sleep out in the garage. Pain leads one down a difficult pathway.

Growing up, Kyle could choose to believe the lies he heard at home about his own character or choose not to be pulled under by them. At the time, when Kyle was my student, I did not know the reason for his tears when he learned he would not be returning to my classroom. Nor did I know the importance of making room for him in my class or the significance behind the four words, "Kyle, you're the man," and his own declaration, "I know I am." Sometimes a person needs to hear the truth and when they hear it, they know it. Kyle heard the truth and when hearing it validated, claimed it for himself.

I did not know dignity, something I assumed he had, was the very thing that had been taken from him. That dignity was now being restored, working within him.

Once again, I see in this reflection, the lies that conspired to separate could not stand against the truth that unites.

Home is carried into school; the good and the bad. Even though I did not know Kyle's background and did not know what he needed, Gracious Inclusion was found to be at work. It cannot be stopped. The need to connect is too strong.

•••

My dad used to say to me, "If you can't have fun, you're done." Kids not only notice what Abe did, but also what he wore. Abe had twelve pairs of Crocs at home, twelve colors, one for each day of the week…fuzzy math, yes, but Abe couldn't have enough of them. And in the eyes of everyone, Abe's Crocs had become institutionalized—wearing them was an integral part of his identity, an icon of his image. The pair he had on would now come into play. It was an orange day. Imaginations ran rampant.

With arms extended, Andrew, who Abe called "Tyrone," because he thought for some strange reason it was funny, came down the hallway at a snail's pace. Andrew's fingers curled around the imaginary handlebars of Danny's painstakingly slow, overweight and underpowered, 1967, Johnson-Evinrude snowmobile that Abe had told him he once owned as a child. "I've got it wide open, Mr. A."

"Slow down, Tyrone!" Abe jokingly commanded. "You'll blow the engine, or the orange skis will fly off." Abe flopped his feet, mimicking a problem, and then kicked off one of his orange Crocs which flew across the hallway. "See, I told you… there one goes right now!" Then Andrew disappeared into the same classroom that Kyle had entered several minutes before.

Donnie, the custodian, pushed a never-ending pile of litter down the hallway. Then he stopped, leaned against a locker and looked at Abe saying, "Don't worry about everything, nothing will be alright." We talked about everything, from family and kids to bad knees, and solving the world's problems, leaving Donnie just enough time to finish sweeping the hallway, and we found nothing was all right. The events in this hall duty were far from being over, as new waves would follow.

Lisa stopped and poured Abe a glass of grape juice that had been left over from an early morning staff meeting. Then Kevin, a fellow science teacher, asked, "Mr. A, can I borrow that Seattle/Tacoma Bridge collapse video?" Abe told Kevin where to find the video of Galloping-Gertie and reminded him to use the resonance tuning forks to describe that phenomenon. Close to the end of his duty time another science teacher came out of her classroom. "Mr. A, Mr. A," Ms. Weeks exclaimed, "come quick into my room." Four wax Dixie cups were supporting the weight of 187 pounds! And with that, Abe's hall duty for the day had ended.

During hall duty, the Five A's were packaged in a ball of yarn and in the reciprocity of Gracious Inclusion others became big in my mind, as I too, became big in theirs. Gracious Inclusion provides a way to think beyond oneself. It is a moving force, and like waves carrying its energy to the shoreline it had surrounded all of us.

Kyle needed to "be the man." And Andrew's humor found resonance with mine as our imaginations put "Tyrone" into the memory of Danny on his Johnson-Evinrude snowmobile. Donnie saw that there was more to being a custodian than pushing a broom. Lisa took time to share a refreshment. While Kevin asked me for something that he could use, Ms. Weeks included me in the excitement of her class's discovery. And a desk, carrying a vulgarity, found useful purpose—connecting teacher with student, who both were searching.

●●●

A Dedication: My friend and custodian, Donnie had retired with me. Upon proofreading this book for final editing, I learned he had passed away. Memories of him taking time with me during my hallway duty will always stay with me.

.

CHAPTER 14

Lock Down

The message crackled over our school P.A. "Take cover, this is a lockdown drill." One quick look down the hallway, no students in sight. Abe locked the door, hit the lights, and now sat with his brood of fifteen hidden in darkness, shielding them from a pretend threat of what or who could be prowling out there. Abe had been this groups homeroom teacher now for four years.

Homeroom, an interesting concept—in this five-minute period of each day the wheels of learning would be set into motion. Before his students would run off to any other subject, Abe was not their science teacher but rather their counselor. He had eyeglasses to see them and wore hearing-aids to hear them, but what to mend a bleeding heart, bathed in a pool of fear? As we waited for the all clear, flashbacks from 55 years ago revisited Danny with more instilled uncertainty.

The Hammer and Sickle of Communism was an icon of fear during the 50s and 60s. Sputnik orbited high overhead, taking pictures of our private lives. Water and canned foods stored in bomb shelters and cellars lay waiting and ready to provide sustenance after the A-bomb was dropped. And yellow civil defense Geiger counters had found their place in schools, where Danny and his classmates practiced hiding under desks which held empty inkwells from the past.

They took shelter from a terrifying future, hoping nuclear fallout from the mushroom clouds they had only seen in news clips would never drop on them—underneath it all, fear was harbored. But Danny's dad, being a WWII Ball Turret Gunner, had taught him well, for they knew who the enemy was, and living in a land sheltered between two oceans, appeared brave. With combination memorized, Danny knew how to quickly unlock the gun cabinet to retrieve his 22 caliber, bolt-action Remington rifle. Oh, he was a dead eye and still owns the dented nickel he had plugged from 20 paces away. Danny even believed an acetylene torch could cut through the wall of the Iron Curtain, setting those captive free.

But fear is a slippery illusion—and Abe would know that he was not alone. For the lessons of fear from long ago had not traveled far. It had crept close—the nemesis, now found in another, was not distanced by any ocean, but a real threat that could break down our classroom door.

With his retirement ready to push him out the same door, Abe sat with his homeroom class in an unlit classroom. They had grown up to be seniors, and throughout the four years together the noise of daily routine had guarded Abe from negative "what if" thoughts. But in the silence, Abe looked at the door wondering if he had really locked it...Knowing students can be lost, Abe thought back, knowing he had been in this position before, unsheltered on the hallway floor, with knees bended, sitting with students all on one level where they grieved classmates who had taken their own lives. Too close from Abe's past the hallway seemed. Pain came back to greet him, "I remember you," it seemed to say, "from me you cannot run, fight or hide." As this reverent reflection passed through the corridors of his mind, Abe tried to shun the dreadful possibility of losing any one of them.

He had never really seen all fifteen of his seniors quite like this before—quiet. For a brief moment in time, the walls of purposeful, carefully crafted agenda crumbled, not to keep fear from coming in, but to push it out. For it had already set up camp residing within them and showed itself in the solemn soberness that was on each face, connecting one to another. Abe had never let his students think it was a disgrace to show their true emotions, especially in their last year together. He had laughed and sometimes cried in front of them.

On their first day as freshmen, he told them that the 700 days of seeing one another would fly by and now it had. For they were only days from graduating, with uncertainties in their own futures. There would no longer be another school year for any of them to look forward to—Abe included. They all would be moving on and knew they would never be together in this one spot again.

The lock-down drill was over, and Abe lifted his protective wing, but his brood did not get up as they normally would have. They remained silent and still, and Abe looked at all of them, saying, "You're in my heart. I lay down my life for you every day." A pause and some eyes watered as his students knew the double meaning behind what had just been spoken. Abe had given his life to this community. For long before they came along, some of their parents had also looked to Abe as their teacher. Time could only separate.

Looking down at his feet, Abe saw a lens that had fallen out of the frame of his glasses—it was not needed in the darkness, for it was with the heart that he had clearly seen. And then unlocking the door, they returned to the noise-filled safety of their daily routine. But for some, the din of daily activities would be no match for the stressor called Chemistry.

CHAPTER 15

Knowing My Students

Gibson was one of Abe's nicest students, but just getting to class some days was an overwhelming challenge for him. Stress knows no boundaries and does not discriminate. It is infectious—viral and can overtake the machinery of our thinking. The subject of science can be threatening and for Gibson the added components of mathematical ratios and stoichiometry made matters worse. He had built emotional roadblocks around his ability to "do science," circumventing cognitive connections, souring his attitude. But today Gibson had made it to class, even on time. He walked over to get a crucible for the day's experiment, pausing to read a poem behind the glass cabinet door.

The Crucible

Dear Class,
The room of Chemistry is a crucible
The crucible can stand the heat but what's inside cannot
Given time, we eventually see the plot.

Things once hidden rise to the surface…
Weaknesses, shortcomings and inadequacies
The stuff we are unable to control reveal a mixture
that we call humanity,
Lying deep within our soul.

Calling on the strength of others,
to help in our time of need
Crying turns to laughter, conceding, we believe.

The colors reveal the stress of life,
Which now is constrained to a new sense of normalcy…
At peace we now remain.

Do not curse the crucible, for it is just a tool
May we all learn to practice the simple Golden Rule.
Gracious in its implement, for some have been
excluded…
We reach out; finally realizing all must be included.

With crucible in hand, Gibson turned to Abe and smiled, knowing he could get the help that he needed. Abe understood that giving students the safety and security of inclusion was an ongoing process. It was about more than what took place within the Chemistry classroom. Transferred to life's problems, Gracious Inclusion would wait to be put to practice. We all need our claim to fame—mine being I knew my students and they knew me.

Abe's Chemistry class had just shuffled in and after taking attendance, he tapped on the board, pointing to the test date. "So, guys, our Chemistry test will be on Friday."

"Mr. Abe," the class grudgingly contested. "We have a huge math test on Friday."

Anxiety escalated. "And that's when our big Psych test is, too," they whined.

"Hmmm," Abe uttered, shutting his eyes and meditating like Yoda, the great Jedi master, and then continued, "you have given me reason for thoughtful reconsideration."

Abe began to chuckle, for the Danny inside recognized the need for immediate action and now with his students sensing the deliberation a mere act, Abe was unable to hide the relief any longer. "Ohhh, stress I see!" Bending his finger like E.T., as he so often did, Abe blurted, "I have absolute power," and with that finger, he touched the whiteboard crossing out the "Test on Friday" date. With empowerment, as if giving life to a dying flower, he proclaimed, "We will preview our new unit on Friday and the test will be on Monday instead."

The students cheered. "Thank you, Mr. Abe."

I could not pinpoint the reason for their elation, and I knew not whether two more days just distanced them from their anticipated doom or gave them more time to study. But I do know concessions connect through emotions and we live in a state of fluctuating perception.

•••

Teaching is filled with life changing opportunity, especially when time is running out and stress is at its peak, as it was for Julie. It was four days before the end of the school year and Julie had not handed in her last lab report. Abe entered a zero into the grade book, dropping her from a passing 60.0% to a failing 59.4%. Abe was bothered by this, for he knew it was his job to reach kids and not fail them. Abe tried to rationalize that some students had handed in all of their assignments over the entire trimester and still only managed to eke out a passing grade. But, Julie had quite a few zeroes in the grade book and bringing her up to their level by giving her a gift would certainly not be right. It was time for Julie to be taught a lesson in responsibility. Abe felt that justice was waiting to be served.

Other teachers had graded the same way, letting students fail, and for years letting it ride. Banging on the door from both sides no one enters, no one leaves; things stay the same.

"I can't help it," Abe said to himself, hitting "save" in the computer's grade-book, before shutting it down. *Would this be a broken record or a record unbroken?* It was simply a matter of cause and effect, and numbers don't lie. But something felt conflicting. Stop—reflect—transform.

With new information, his perception would change, no longer fooled—Abe had come to his senses. Julie had lost her grandmother the week before. An email from Julie's counselor made Abe aware that Julie had been struggling with this anticipated loss for a long time. He began to rethink. If a chicken thinks there's a coyote outside, opening the door would never be safe, and maybe for Julie the door was tightly locked. Abe now knew what was needed.

The next day Julie walked in with the class. Abe sat down next to Julie at her desk. He let her know he was aware of her struggle, but she needed the points from the missing lab report to pass, and these words poured out, "Julie, I don't want you to fail. You can have more time. Do you need help?" Julie would no longer be in lock-down mode.

Realizing she was not alone with her feelings, she spoke, "Mr. Abrahamson, I think I'll be OK, I understand the assignment. I am able get it in tomorrow." Julie was at the start of regaining her very own security. For reaching the affective domain had spring boarded up into cognitive recruitment, showing her thoughts were heading from the cellar of despair up to a new way of thinking about Abe as her teacher, the class, herself, and the assignment.

The next day, Julie handed in her lab report. Awake and aware of Julie's struggles, Abe was able to acknowledge, accept, and accommodate her needs instead of ignoring them and letting her fail. Putting to practice the 5 A's of Gracious Inclusion is about more than just getting a passing grade.

After school, Abe had time to read Julie's assignment. It was clear and articulate, and at the end Julie left a note signed fully with her first, middle, and last name saying, "Thanks Mr. Abe, you found me."

Upon that note he cried.

CHAPTER 16

Obstinacy, A Science Lesson

The difference between boiling an egg or a potato is the outcome…both sit in the same hot water, but one gets hard and the other gets soft. And it makes me wonder what happens in the cooking pot of life.

It had been years since visiting Gene down in Iowa. No longer in Mason City, he had moved 150 miles farther south, to be close to his grandkids, carrying every rusty-dusty piece of junk from his hobby-farm with him. It was as if his entire farm had been transported—untouched, miraculously preserved.

"Don't laugh," Gene said to me as he opened the sliding door of the machine shed which was the size of a small barn.

There lay all the junk, like an unfinished puzzle that he had stopped working on long ago. In my mind I was not able to reserve judgement. Why would this old man not throw at least one rusty screw or broken car jack away? Even with my eyes closed I could tell it was his place. The sweet semi-musty smell of cut grass glued to the undercarriage of his

John Deere blended with the faint smell of transmission oil stains.

Gene could read what I was thinking and was quick to justify. "You know, Dan, I'll live into my mid-nineties." I would not condemn, for I knew what it meant to hang on to things that were old and sometimes broken—after all, you have to have something laying around the place in need of fixing. Even though I carried a "AAA" card, I still had a leaky hydraulic jack at home that was of value or at least could be of use—someday. And in my wallet, I still carry a picture of my children from 27 years ago. Out of fear we don't let go, wishing for things to remain the same.

Late into the night, old friends talked, picking up on conversations as if 40 years were only yesterday. The next morning Gene's wife asked me, "Dan, why did you change?"

"I don't know," I said. "I just did."

Change happens.

•••

The egg slammed against the chalkboard with a loud, "Crack!"

"Why did the egg break?" Abe asked his students as they shriveled their noses. Yellow ooze slid down the wall as broken shells lay at the foothill of destructive inertia. Abe continued to prod. "Don't look at the egg, but the wall." Students shook their heads. "The egg broke because the wall didn't want to move."

Then using a single thread that Abe had stolen from his wife's sewing basket he hung a weight from the ceiling and attached another similar thread to the bottom of the weight dangling as a tail.

"If I grab the tail and snap it down toward the floor, which of the two threads will break? The tail or the thread holding the weight to the ceiling?"

Abe's students clamored, "The thread attached to the ceiling because it is holding all the weight."

Abe yanked on the tail, and it broke as it had all the other times he had previously taught this lesson, at the bottom, leaving the stubborn resistance unaffected. The weight still clung to the thread hanging from the ceiling.

Encouraging an applause as if he had just performed a great magical act, Abe bowed and then extending his arm pointed to the miracle, explaining, "Like the wall, the weight did not want to move. And the tail, like the egg, experienced destructive inertia. Both broke." Now hooked, Abe dug deeper.

"How can I pull on the tail and get the thread that attaches the weight to the ceiling to break?"

"Well, you have to do something different," Abe's curious students replied.

Patting himself on the back Abe said, "Yes, good scientific thinking—you have been trained well. Do something different for different results."

Abe thought of the times over the years when he had become impatient and unwilling to wait, only to be destroyed by the resistance of an unruly class or a system too great for him to move. And now it would be his students' turn.

Abe once again pointed to the weight still hanging from the ceiling and said, "Think of something in your life that is too big for you to handle or overcome." Abe paused and then started to slowly pull on the tail of the thread as if stretching taffy. "It takes time and patience, but slowly the weight, which wants to stay at rest, will be encouraged to move, always breaking the thread attached to the ceiling."

And with that said, the thread broke, sending the resistance free-falling to the floor. "We are all products of change over time."

"But what if we don't have the patience or time?" A student asked.

"There is a way to speed things up."

Abe reattached the weight to the ceiling and added five threads to the bottom of the weight. Moving around the room, Abe looked into their eyes and asked them to write about a problem in their life that they would like to move or have changed.

Thinking showed on their faces and they wrote in their journals. Like finger painting in Kindergarten, making meaningful connections was a classroom activity all students could do. Abe had a poster hanging on his wall which said, "MMC: Make Meaningful Connections" and students used their journals to connect lessons to their personal experiences. Making their own connections was non-threatening, for there was no right or wrong answer.

"Now," Abe inquired, "what threads will be needed to get the resistance in your life to move?"

Rather than only copying notes from the chalkboard, students were proud of the connections made in their MMC journals, for these were their own.

Abe then quickly pulled down, using all five threads to overcome the resistance—sending the weight crashing to the floor. The strength of the five threads combined allowed for this to happen. The strength of using the Five A's, also allows for conflicting resistance to move. Using these five does not change things for you, but instead changes you for things.

•••

Over the years, chalkboards would be replaced by smartboards, but for Abe, the review time for some units seemingly couldn't be helped by technology and remained deadly.

No lab today, just a boring review lecture, whose painful delivery had anesthetized Abe's first hour class. For years, he had hated the review part of this unit.

Here I go again... Abe thought. Could he really do this all day? But that's just the way it was—once set, change is resisted. Second hour class was squirming in their chairs, and Abe envisioned buzzards circling around his corpse by half-time. He looked at them. They were sleeping with their eyes open. In fact, some were actually closing!

"And so, class," *Blah, blah, blah...yes, it was going to be one of those days.* Abe looked up at the banner, which always advertised the vigilant reminder, "MMC: Make Meaningful Connection... Tying the New to the Known," something he had not asked his students to do the hour before.

In midstream Abe realized his horse couldn't swim, and now he was the one who closed his eyes. Then out of a long breath of *Chutes Away* he began to sing his chosen song of deliverance, "We all live in a yellow submarine..."

Changing course, Abe turned to another file in his computer—throwing it on the smartboard, he instructed them, "Okay guys, read this story. After reading, give the story a title."

"Sally first tried setting lose a team of gophers. The plan backfired when a dog chased them away. She then entertained a group of teenagers and was delighted when they brought motorcycles. Unfortunately, she failed to find a Peeping Tom listed in the Yellow Pages. Furthermore, her stereo system was not loud enough. The crab grass might have worked, but she didn't have a fan that was sufficiently powerful. The obscene phone calls gave her hope until the number was changed. She thought about calling a door-to-door salesperson, but she decided to hang up a clothes line instead. It was the installation of the blinking neon lights across the street that did the trick. She eventually framed the ad from the classified section." (Anonymous)

Students shared their possible titles for the story as Abe wrote them on the board, telling them not to be too frustrated. While Sally seemed to be crazy, she really was a smart little gal—all that was needed was a connector to see how it made perfect sense.

Abe shared the title, "Getting Rid of The Neighbors." Now that students knew what Sally was really up to, he had them reread the story while connecting the content to the title.

Life needs titles—meaningful connections that provide insight. Life needs meaningful connections.

Abe returned to the unit review with MMC in mind. He shared some of his connections to the content of the unit and asked students to do the same for themselves.

●●●

We can stare at something for so long that we fail to open our minds to a new way of thinking. Obsessed with our focus we can be fooled into seeing something that is really not there.

Take a look at the image below. Are there really dots at each intersection? Or is it only an illusion?

While looking at the illusive dots think of all the people in your life, the ones who are hard to deal with, the ones who push your buttons—a school board who won't negotiate, a co-worker who won't collaborate, or a student refusing to do the work. Think of those demanding all of your attention and pushing you to the point of exhaustion, interfering with your willingness to put the 5 A's of Gracious Inclusion to practice. So, how do we get across this grid with so many dots blocking the way?

Continue to look at the grid and refocus. Focus on one intersection at a time and Poof! the dot disappears. Perhaps it is not about the bully, but about you and your own struggles, unresolved issues, conflicts, and inability to focus. Stopping at one of the 5 A's puts a roadblock in Gracious Inclusion. Getting across the grid without any roadblocks happens one intersection at a time.

I was tired and burnt out. Perhaps you are also at the point in your life of being willing to change. We are part of something bigger than ourselves. When overwhelmed, refocus. Change happens one "A" at a time, until we see all 5 A's working together, getting us across the intersection of each new situation.

Over the course of my teaching, I had run the gauntlet, seeing broken egg shells, never thinking to consider the wall that did not want to move, or the string that always broke in the wrong spot. When I became stalled in my teaching, I knew Abe needed to do something different to get different results. Knowing what to look for takes time to stop, reflect, and ask, "Which one of the Five A's am I having trouble with?" And at times, the weight still hangs from the ceiling.

CHAPTER 17

Stupid

Abe gave his best and expected the best—believing in kids. Today, the subject of Chemistry would expose not only academic strengths but weaknesses. Abe had always let emotions freely fly in his classroom and he was up on the high road, throwing caution to the wind. Maybe things had gotten too familiar.

Twenty minutes into the dialogue of Chemistry review and the train was cruising with a full head of steam. The test was the next day and smack dab in the middle of a key idea with high hopes, Abe asked all those onboard, "So then, what information is needed to change moles to grams?"

There always seemed to be at least one student who was not with the program. "What chapter are we in?" Darcy rudely interrupted, knocking Abe's train of thought off its tracks.

A bell in his head went *Ding!* as he fired back in knee-jerk response, "Now, that's a stupid question." Abe saw right through Darcy's smoke-screened admission that she was not bothered by being lost. It was as if she wanted to publicly gloat that she hadn't felt it worthwhile to look at a damn thing. And Abe, convinced that this was a challenge that threatened a trust in the value of education and hard work, did not have any patience for such nonsense. He would be damned if he didn't publicly call her on it. The crucible of chemistry had heated up, changing the class into a courtroom.

In his mind Abe knew he didn't have far to go to set up a defense that would exonerate him. Chapter 9 had been written on the board for the last two weeks. Materials had been given out with Chapter 9 clearly written on the top of the page. Chapter 9 questions with an answer sheet and directives to chapter illustrations had almost been spoon fed to them since starting the unit two weeks ago.

Abe would not let one student insult the hard work of others by trying to undermine the integrity of education. He would fight to protect his keep as he immediately went into pursuit mode. "Read the board!" Abe resounded.

"I can't read the board," Darcy bantered, pushing Abe's buttons with an annoying whine.

"Do you need glasses?" Abe whined in return, cornering Darcy with her lame excuse, even though walking past the board every day, Darcy claimed that she could not read what had been printed on it.

All this rational within a split second raced through Abe's head and yet how could he, a seasoned teacher, close to retirement, have used the word "stupid"? Within the same breath, with fuel vaporizing close to its flash point, Abe recognized his entrapment and sensed the onset of a lynching. Peers conformed to their roles, being caught up in the power of the situation at hand and Abe was doomed. Now, the whole class was not with him, but on the side of the offended party—the teacher stood alone and began back-peddling.

"It was the question that was stupid," Abe recanted, "you are not." But the transfer of stupid had already struck its mark and trying to stop the bleeding was like using a Band-Aid for a tourniquet.

Blood was in the water and it was Abe's own. He became frenzied in his feeble attempt to defend his position, stumbling in deliberation. Then Abe's painful dissertation was mercifully interrupted by a voice from another student who exuded an admirable make-it-better personality—which was a necessary relief valve for the pressure-cooker-environment that squeezed out both the best and, at times, the worst in all of us. Ironically, Abe had nick-named her "Crabby" because of her never-ending cheerful disposition, and in the context of the classroom's usual joking atmosphere, the play on the name was one she really liked.

"Mr. Abrahamson, all you need to say is that you're sorry." Crabby's comment, trying to give reprieve, cut into Abe like a reprimand.

"Crabby, you sound like my daughter, telling me to apologize to mom." Knowing her to be right, Abe then turned and publicly apologized. "Darcy, I am sorry." Eating crow sticks in your craw…it was dry and hard to swallow. Abe somehow knew he would not be so easily vindicated.

The next day the assistant principal came down to Abe's class informing him that Darcy's mom had called the office. An appointment had been set up to meet with Darcy and her mom at the end of the day. Abe had never met this parent and was anxious not only to set things straight, but to get down to the bottom of what was really happening and come up with a plan that would help Darcy better understand Chemistry. Abe told Darcy that he would share this plan with her and her mom.

Later that day, Darcy's mom called into the office, canceling the appointment—never talking to Abe. His disappointment added to his frustration, and yet, Abe still met with Darcy and gave her a formal apology in the presence of the assistant principal and made suggestions for academic improvement.

The air had been cleared as heart-felt feelings were expressed and then handshakes and smiles were exchanged. He felt relieved, but this would still not be the end of it.

The next morning before school, Bill, the head principal came down to Abe's room. "Dan," Bill's voice took on his low tone, official resonance. "I need to meet with you at the end of the day. If you would like to have a union representative in this meeting, you should invite one to join us."

Abe felt powerless, and as if Danny had just been told by his mother to "wait until your father gets home," Abe worried about what his punishment would be. Abe's thoughts were once again derailed. The first hour bell rang and as students trickled into class, Abe knew he would not be able to have a wonderful day of teaching.

Danny would put a newspaper inside his drawers when expecting a spanking from his father. And at day's end, as suggested, Abe decided to bring Carrie, a union representative, into the meeting for what was assumed to be protective cover—which would make good padding as the meeting was soon to ramp up into more threatening intimidation.

The building principal slid a paper across the table to him, mumbling something Abe did not hear because what was printed on that page spoke to him too loudly. Under the school's letterhead in bold print was "Tennessen Warning: NOTICE TO EMPLOYEE." The warning continued, saying, "The purpose of this meeting is to discuss allegations of improper behavior by you and that the information collected may be used by the School District…in termination, suspensions or other disciplinary proceedings and may be used in civil litigation." There was a place for a signature below. Abe's heart began to pound.

How could I be treated like this? Abe thought. *Was this not the same district that when I applied, in 1981, did not even have an application form or contract for me to sign?* Back then trust was in a hand shake and a pay check in the P.O. Box once a month was good enough. But now, they certainly had a pen for Abe and had thrown it across the table as trust was being breached by a warning filled with words not defining the ideals of the district he once knew and thought were still in place. When and how did this happen? Abe had given his life to this community.

Still thinking in defiance, Abe tried to justify his feelings, *Didn't they know this was me…the only teacher who had been bold enough to march in the homecoming parade?* No, they did not know. The district had grown too large for homecoming buttons, too large for having a parade, too large to remember being small.

Shell-shocked, Abe stared at the paper and in his confusion fired back a cry for help meant to be heard throughout the school. "I'm not going to sign this damn thing! Do I need to get a lawyer?"

"That is your choice," the principal responded with dead pan expression. "You are under a lot of stress." Abe felt as if being pushed into a box, and in this box, there would be room for only one boss. The rebel in Abe stirred.

"Do you like doing this?" Abe asked.

"No."

"Then, stop," Abe demanded. "This is not right."

How could friend turn foe? And like a dog that had now turned into a wolf, fear was circling his camp. Conflicted, he ran from the very place that for more than half of his life had given him protection.

Once again, fear-to-love waited to be expressed, and at home my PTSD was triggered as I experienced seizures that very night. While asleep, I had a dream—an elevator door was closing, hearing quickening footsteps, a finger pressed the door's "stay open" button. And then I awoke, not knowing which, the finger, or footsteps, were mine. I no longer knew if I was the one giving the help or needing the help for myself.

Gracious Inclusion works, for it is reciprocating, and now awakened, I would put to practice the other four "A's." Aware of my conundrum and ready to acknowledge, accept and accommodate—so simple it seemed to just see, greet, smile and open the door, but not easy when pride had been put in the wrong place. Both Danny and Abe had always looked for a chance to be kind and being so foul had put me in a place that I did not wish to be.

Abe had never been able to let go and trust things would be okay without his intervention. This mindset had been transferred to his students, and by this same pathway, it had been transferred to Bill. Error in thinking held Abe captive as it did now with the injustice he perceived.

He had learned long ago a lack of trust would only lead to micro-management, frustration, anger, and destroyed relationships. And now, it was not his students, but Bill who Abe thought had a grip on him…Abe was choking, for he had forgotten his lesson.

Misconceived notions once again conspired to bind him—they hid behind a mask of fear that Abe now wore—a mask that had laid abandoned long ago on the shoulder of a lonely highway. He returned to his classroom, his place of refuge, to reflect on the situation.

So familiar was this feeling, as the expanding force to unite pushed against the compression for control. When Danny had been bullied by Benny, he thought, *"How could Benny ever be someone's friend?"* Then later, he saw Benny knocked out and through a welcomed flip in polarities, although Danny feared him, he had come to Benny's rescue. How close this was to the time when Abe's world was spinning, and Bill came down to the nurse's office out of concern for him.

Yet now came an unwanted flip in polarities, changing Bill from friend to foe. Abe then decided to go to Bill first, and not wait for him to come to his rescue. Abe knew this to be right, for immediately after moving with this unifying force of Gracious Inclusion, instead of against it, he was at peace and felt as if lifted off that cold, damp cement floor. Fourteen hours after that nightmarish incident I sent this email:

Dear Bill,

I start with dear for this is a note of tenderness. I have had time to process. As I reflect back on our meeting yesterday, I remember seeing the concern in my friend, Carrie's eyes, while words between us were spoken. She was worried for me. Seeing that emotion changed my way of thinking and so here are some of my thoughts.

The nicest thing you said to me was "you are under a lot of stress." That statement was so powerful and stuck in my mind; it showed me something about you. You have empathy.

Then I asked myself, "why am I under all of this stress?" I was afraid, worried about losing control, fearing the unknown...not knowing what or why something was happening. This was all too familiar to me.

Fear gives three options...To run, fight or hide. I love all of those here at STMA and so I could not run away, and I may seem at times to be a fighter, but that is not in my character and am conflicted by it. I cannot live nor breathe in conflict, for in it, I will be "bled and no longer fed" by the very life I have here.

So, I have decided to run to and not away from my fear-to-love... I trust you as my boss and am happy to come to work today.

Changed by tears,
Dan Abrahamson

It was not Bill, but Abe who needed changing. Once again Gracious Inclusion had shown its power, for Abe had been the wolf all along, now turned into shepherd.

CHAPTER 18

Crayons

School can be ruined—becoming no longer a place where we want to be, but a place that is filled with hurt and insecurity. Abe knew that the cherished childhood memories of many had been deeply buried under the lies that sought to separate. Lies such as: "You're too little," "too big," "just plain stupid," "unworthy," or "not one of us." It was these untruths that had left them behind, forgotten. Abe needed to bring them back—all back, to a time when smiles did abound. But how?

Doris came into the first day of High School Biology class loudly. Rocking back in her chair, spinning around to survey who was there, she sprang to her feet and pointed across the room. "Whaaat's uuuup?" Her voice boomed.

"You're a spark plug," Abe said, being pulled into the vortex. "Every day I want you to get out of your desk, walk over to the menu on the door, and read to the class in your loudest voice what's for lunch."

"Can I do it right now?" Doris begged. Abe pointed to the door and nodded.

After Doris finished, she returned to her desk smiling and sat down. With Doris wanting to be the center of the universe, Abe poured more energy into the whirlpool. "Doris, I am going to put this ice cream bucket under your sniffer. Close your eyes, smell, and tell me what's in the bucket."

Closing her eyes, Doris wrinkled her nose. Memories are sometimes soft. "Crayons," she whispered. Abe then told Doris to hand out some crayons to everyone.

"Class," Abe instructed. "Smell a crayon and tell the person next to you the name of your Kindergarten teacher and what you liked about school." I thought of Miss Latt and broke out into the song "Big Eyed Rabbit." The whole class was abuzz.

Abe gave them a blank piece of paper and continued. "Using the crayons and your non-writing hand, draw a picture showing what life looks like to you."

"But what do we draw?" Students asked.

"You are free, anything you like."

Out flowed flowers, clouds, doggies, big people, little people, tanks, rockets, and stars. As the class colored their pictures, their faces contorted with a myriad of expressions—life is not always filled with smiles. In his own mind, Abe drew a picture of Danny walking up the driveway, holding momma's hand, and smiling at "them bees." Abe then told his students to use their non-writing hands to print their names.

Abe proudly displayed his name on the board, a perfect match from what he remembered. The kindergartner is always in you. Confusion then settled in. "Mr. A, what are we going to do with these pictures?"

"Well," Abe said. "Bring them home, walk up to your mom or dad with your picture hiding behind your back. Get really close to their face so you 'break their bubble' and just smile, say nothing until they say something. They will probably ask, 'How was your first day at school?' That's when you unveil your beautiful masterpiece and proudly hold it right up to their noses." Students looked at Abe as if he had crabs crawling on his face.

Hank, a burly student, gave a child-like inquiry showing sensitivity and wonder. He stuttered a little and asked, "Wha-wha-what do you think our parents will do?"

"They'll throw them in the garbage," another student huffed, making Hank cower and feel small.

"Dah, no they won't…" Doris knowingly exclaimed, using her overbearing demeanor to provide protective cover, "…they'll put it on the refrigerator, of course."

"Yes," Abe interjected. "Make sure your parents put them on the refrigerator. Leave them up for one week, secretly recording the comments your family makes and then bring your picture back to class and tell me what this has taught you."

A week had passed and Abe collected the crayon pictures with their comments. After giving his students credit, they were all returned with a star next to each of their names.

Doris looked around at the pictures and announced, "We all got stars."

The smell of crayons brought our class back to the point before the growing pains of adolescence. For a brief moment, my students had returned to a memory—when their kindergarten teacher put a star on the top of everyone's paper. It was a time when work was not thrown in the garbage, but instead brought home and proudly shared. Believing it was of great value, the work was displayed for all to see, and later stored by a parent in the archives of a kindergarten folder to be saved and then opened once again for display twelve years later upon the day of graduation; a moment captured in time. Kindergarten was a time when everything was new—a place where nothing was stupid and a time when we could all say, "I like school."

CHAPTER 19

Magic Seeds

I believe in the power that breathes life into a seed. Seeds grow, for they have received nutrients. Before coming into my classroom to make a formal observation, my principal would always give me a heads-up and say, "Dan, I'll be coming in next week to see you work your magic." This year, there would be no need for an official observation because of my upcoming retirement, but I still had magic to give.

Kids really want to believe in magic, and year after year got caught up in an old teacher's dream—a dream that bald is beautiful, Crocs are meant to be worn every day, and that there are seeds that look like Cheerios that will grow donut trees…

Over 36 years, more than 7,500 students had graced Abe's classroom and every year he gave each of his students a packet of Cheerios telling them, "These seeds are magic. Plant them and document your scientific procedure as the seeds will germinate and grow donuts."

It warmed Abe's heart to give magic donut seeds to a second generation of students and hear how it made their parents laugh and say, "I see Mr. Abe is up to his magic again." Year after year students always brought back photographic evidence and statements as documentation.

One student's testimony bore witness to the fact that the magic really did work, "At first I was skeptical, but then I was dumbfounded to awaken to a full-sized Donut Bush! They sure were great." Proof of the magic was undeniable as students returned to class with more evidence—freshly grown donuts that had to be eaten. The donut seeds had become iconic.

Several months before graduation Abe asked Bill permission to speak to the graduating class as they assembled in order to be prepped before commencement. Bill thought this to be a good idea, seeing as Abe would be retiring at the end of the year and they were all on their way out together.

The day of the assembly came and Abe, also preparing for his own retirement, addressed the graduating Class of 2015, sharing packets of magic seeds one last time, along with a poem for each senior.

STMA "2015" Magic Donut Seeds

Don't you want a donut bush
Or
How about a tree
All you have to do is plant these seeds

Keeping them will not do
You have to let them go
Dig and prod, now sow

Come back in time and you will see
Kids and trees mark time, I believe in magic
Thank you for believing in me

Where to Plant: Where your heart leads you
When to Plant: When you are afraid
How to Plant: Close your eyes; throw seeds in circles
Care: Water with belief
Ingredients: Hope mixed with Trust

Abe had prepared them, as well as himself for the change that lay ahead. As he passed out the magic donut seeds, he told them, "Believe. You can become anything you dream to be." All that remained were seeds of grandiose idealistic thinking, and you know—that was all that was ever needed, because seeds are planted and grow.

The magic is to believe—it is invisible, but the results are not. It is the glue that keeps us together, giving us hope. It fills us with expectation for continuation as we trust in interdependencies that connect us to something bigger than ourselves.

CHAPTER 20

Why Now? You Have to be Kidding Me!

Thirteen days left until Abe would walk away from his classroom domain where he had been transformed and now two quizzes lay under his red pen next to each other with identically incorrect answers. Instinctively he stopped, no need to continue correcting their other answers; two red zeroes decorated the top next to their names. *Why now?* Abe thought, *I'm supposed to be retiring.*

Abe showed the quizzes to another teacher, who confirmed his first instinct. "Yep, no doubt." Mr. Z smirked, "Seen this before…Cheaters!" Abe was bound to not let it go unnoticed.

Here I go again, Abe thought as he dialed one of the student's home phone numbers. On the other end, Abe heard something that had been said to him so many times before: "That doesn't sound like my child," the parent exclaimed.

"Please have them stop in tomorrow before school and explain," Abe responded.

The next morning the students came into Abe's classroom and stood silently before him.

"Well?" Abe prodded. They remained silent. "Tell me about the quiz."

"We didn't cheat," they rang out in unison. Sharing the evidence, Abe gave them another chance for them to come clean. And yet they once again chimed, "We didn't cheat."

"That's Bull-Shit!" Abe countered. "Now you're not only cheating but lying...follow me to the office."

Three hours were added to an already packed and busy teaching day, through a volley of e-mails, phone calls, and ultimately conflicting positions—it was "us versus them," as a wall of obstinate positions separated school and family. Gridlock. A meeting was set up for 9 o'clock the next morning.

Nobody needed to tell Abe when they arrived, sometimes you hear trouble before you can see it, and now they were barreling down the tracks fueled by emotional drama surpassing the momentum of a runaway freight train. Abe felt tied to the tracks and unable to get away with everything in slow motion.

The parents fumed into the room. Yet before information could fly out Abe was quick to give an apology for his lapse in professional articulation. He cleared his throat to deliver a speech that was eloquently crafted to be more suited to the point. "I should not have called something so close to your children 'bull-shit,' and instead of saying they were lying, I should have said the evidence conflicts with their insistence on not cheating. And for that I ask for your forgiveness."

These parents did not know Abe and he refused to be intimidated by their examination of his character. He would not be bullied but wishing for vindication he would allow himself to be placed on a psychiatric couch, delving into a forensic endeavor to celebrate his role as an advocate for truth. For a moment, Abe pondered, *Why? What makes me share the inner workings of my mind? Shouldn't I instead just be laying on a beach for retirees? I thought I was ready to walk away into the sunset.* Then Abe was back to being judged.

In rebuttal, the opposition fired a zinger at him, putting Abe on the spot, "What kind of half-assed teacher are you?" Abe crossed his once open arms. He so wanted to be someplace else. He looked to Bill.

The principal handed the quizzes in question to the parents and tried to show with unbiased objectivity the evidence that was before them.

Both answers for Question #3 (6.233×10^{-11}) screamed off their pages with no calculations shown; they were just identically wrong and with explanations misspelled exactly the same way. Each one read: "No eye-ons precipitate. They won't fall out of salution." The chances of winning the lottery were better than this coming out of two noggins working independently.

Not even looking at the evidence, the parents pushed the quizzes away. "Our kids don't cheat." It was all for not, and one of Paul Simon's old songs immediately echoed in Abe's brain, *"All lies and jest, still a man hears what he wants to hear and disregards the rest."* Abe almost started singing

147

the words out loud, but instead it would be Abe's words that pierced the heart of the matter.

With pointed finger, Abe tapped twice on the table pinning the quizzes down the second time as if he had caught a mouse by the tail. Leaning forward, he countered, "Maybe I need to include the Athletic Director in this discussion." And then suddenly it was quiet. The students, who were star athletes, were soon to be playing in the State Tournament and both expected college scholarships. Like deer in the darkness of night, everyone sat frozen, not knowing whether it was safe to move right or left, so they just stayed.

Abe had assumed control, but now the stakes had been raised and the wall between school and family had become ever taller. Aware of the repercussions and not wishing to ruin a life, nor to put the integrity of education in jeopardy, Abe would need to find a way to knock that wall down, so they could be connected. It seemed an eternity to get to the other side of grid-lock, and then from a whisper of thought that built to a crescendo Abe exclaimed, "I've got it...I'll give the girls' quizzes the same percent they get on the test today. Then it won't be a zero. That way they can show me what they really know!"

It was not the principal, not the parent, not the student... it was Abe, the teacher, in the position of power. Abe needed to find the crack in the wall to make it tumble down and out of a pile of rubble a donut tree would grow. And so, there everyone sat—as one.

As he got out of his chair and started to leave the students followed Abe like a pair of ducklings. He gave each girl a package of donut seeds. "Carry them with you. Read the message tonight with your parents. I will see you both next hour. Nail that test." Abe had given them a gift—Gracious Inclusion works all the time.

Before they departed in the hallway, high fives were exchanged. "Thanks Mr. Abe. Thanks for everything."

Once he got back to the classroom, Abe shot a quick e-mail to Bill, "The heart knows the way. Thank you."

Ten minutes later Bill came down to his room, "Abe, it was your turn and you did the right thing."

"What was that?" Abe searched for his answer.

"Hope," Bill emphatically imprinted. "You gave them hope. Everyone left knowing."

Mix hope with trust and water those seeds, believing— it's so simple and when it happens it is magical.

CHAPTER 21

Letting One Go...From Shart to Finish

Thirty-six years, and I have trouble saying this will be my last. But I want to leave while I'm at the top of my game. While people are still saying, "don't leave" rather than "why the hell ya still here?" Abe was a tangential coot, who saw the value of putting a shine on a red apple, seeing every face, and knowing what cards he had in his hand and when to play them. Never needing to open a notebook to see where he was in his lessons, he knew where he stood.

Yes, Abe had morphed...free-lancing and free-wheeling, responsive to cognitive and emotional needs while monitoring and adjusting in mid-flight. Having fun—the time of his life. And now I am taken back to the beginning when all things were new and so unpredictable.

It was the first day of my teaching career, back in Iowa. Pressure mounted, peristaltic movement ran rampant, and the basement of my bowels began to gurgle. Between classes, when I thought all was safe, I let one rip—it was a shart: a shit-fart. I had soiled my trousers.

My students always laughed when I told them this story and insisted it be included in this book. So, I share this story, not to be crude, but to conform to their liking, and as a reminder to lighten up—at least you don't have shit in your pants. Like so many other events that would fill my teaching career, what happened that day was beyond my control.

I have written, sometimes smiling and sometimes crying, in reflection. But how would I know when it was time to retire? Omens, please, do tell.

●●●

Fall 2012: Tomorrow would be the 176th day of my 700 days with my last group of homeroom students, and it would be their first day as sophomores. Earlier that day, some of them had painted four ominous numbers on the ends of the sophomore locker pods just outside my room. "2 0 1 5." Like a neon sign the numbers flashed, speaking to me. It was a voice from above saying, "Leave with them!"

I felt as if Abe once again was standing alone in a dark parking lot looking at the stars, searching for something. And now with no sign of life and the corridors empty, I looked up the stairwell and whimsically hollered, "Yes, Bill. I hear you!"

●●●

Fall 2015: Cagan had always been there, in the same building, hitting the same nail on the head, convincing kids that they were worth it. Likewise, convincing me that, I too, maybe wasn't crazy, staying. And now after 34 years of teaching with this man, we found ourselves old, both having health issues.

The next morning before school revved up, I sauntered into his room to check on him. The room was empty except for one student and Mr. Cagan who sat glued to his chair. "You know Cagan, I really don't need this place."

"Ya, right," he knowingly chuckled.

Cagan's eyes followed me as I walked to the back of his room where an archive of forty social study documentaries lay stored in their original metal canisters, labeled "Return Promptly to County Library" with yellowing tape covering faded due dates. It could only be another old fart like Abe who would see value in these. No one else wanted them. I placed my finger on the back wheel of the reel to reel projector that now had become so obsolete it should have been discarded with the IBM ball typewriters thirty years ago—funny how we hang onto things. The wheel lay empty, waiting for its next 16 mm feed. Spinning the wheel, I spouted, "What are you going to do with this dinosaur?"

"You or the projector?" Cagan retorted.

"Both," I sat down and looked at him. "Is the diuretic working on your swollen ankles?" Cagan pulled up his pant legs. I shook my head, grunting, "Damn, you'd better get out of here with me."

"No, Abe...I can't."

I gave him a hug, feeling the importance of routine and the safety it provided. Just like Cagan's old reels, memories clicked and projected on the screen in my own mind and then hearing its ticking, I looked at the clock, realizing, "Gosh...time to teach, got to rock and roll." I returned to the relics of my own room that had accumulated over three decades. It would be hard to let go.

•••

February 2015: At the beginning of our final year, I had told my homeroom seniors that I was getting the heck out of here with them. And now the school year was two-thirds over. We had just torn off day "63" from our count down sign; only 62 student contact days remained. I had decided that today would be a special day for making my intended departure from this profession official, for it was my birthday: February 26th. And I, at 62 years of age, being partially dyslectic, was quite fittingly tickled by the flip-flop interplay between these two numbers. I considered the alignment of these three sets of numbers—62, 26, 62—on this particular day to be another omen.

During my first hour prep, I had just written a formal letter for leaving my position. My letter did not use the "R" word, for I had always attached retirement to old people that were just one step away from actually leaving this planet, and I certainly wasn't ready to have February 26, 1953-2015 sandblasted into the granite of a tombstone.

I hadn't signed the letter yet and was reluctant—always envisioning this moment as if being pushed off a dock into a lake of icy cold water, and now I was at the end of the dock still not realizing what was happening. What I was about to do would be final, for it would deliver closure to what I knew was inevitable. My time had come.

With unsigned letter in hand, I took my first step out of the classroom and then I heard voices, "Hey, Mr. A." It was three of my homeroom students coming out of another science room, "We're going to our lockers." I sensed an appointment, not controlled by me but one tailor-made long ago, waiting and now ready. "Where are you going?" They asked.

Funny, I thought. *They stopped me with the question of destination and not one of what I was doing.* "I'm going to give my…" I didn't have to finish. Tears were already in my eyes as they looked into me, they knew.

"We'll take you there." How did they know my legs were weak and my decision wavering? And take me they did, carrying me on wings-like-angels up to the front door of the office. I began to thank them and raised my hand to bid them farewell. They shook their heads as they opened the door for me, "We're going in with you."

My boss was at the reception desk, talking to two of the secretaries. I looked at Bill saying, "It is time." I picked up the pen that lay there and signed the letter, in front of a witness of couriers who, now with me, were crying. This was not as I had imagined, for I felt I had not been pushed into a lake of freezing water but was surrounded by flowing waters warmed from hearts of love.

"Mr. Abe," my angels sang. "We're not done."

"Where are you taking me?" Thinking it couldn't get any better. "To Heaven?"

"No, to Mr. Cagan."

"Oh, we're going to Hell," I chuckled, as I knew what they were up to.

Mr. Cagan sang "Happy Birthday" to me in his shrill off-key manner, breaking out into a trade-marked falsetto finale to an applauding audience of students. You know, Hell's not bad...especially when you get a birthday song and a hug out of it.

We returned to where we had started and I looked at these three and thanked them, knowing that they had done what I was not able to do. They had carried me beyond my dreams. As they returned to their class, in my mind I heard singing.

●●●

As a teacher, I was able to do something about the "Timmys" with pee-soaked trousers, kids with dented Zorro lunch boxes, little red-haired girls with buck teeth, and campers with stripped dignity. I was able to see their need, for I had been changed.

Not forgetting the bully, I saw the threatening fists that once alienated change to open hands that welcomed high-fives instead. I saw the "Posts," thought to be losers become winners because inclusion was stronger than exclusion. And in Abe, my students found Danny, with all of his insecurities, shortcomings, hopes and dreams. Reciprocity works.

The plans in my life had been so carefully glued together and my classroom had become a museum of my teaching career, having gone years without one staple or artifact being removed. And now, at the end of my career, I would be forced to clean it all out, throwing so much away, for there was no room to take it all home, save a few special items.

For one last time, Abe with Danny looked into the concave mirror which hung at the back of the classroom. *Bald is Beautiful,* Abe thought as he read the inscription, in a student's handwriting, surrounding the mirror. He had faced his own insecurities and inadequacies, found humor in embarrassment, and saw "Posts" transformed back into students as their labels fell off. Abe was able to find a way to reach them.

Yes, I was afraid of leaving this place, but would never be separated from those and that which I love. Show me a man who does not fear and I'll show you a man who has lost his love. But that would not be me. So, out from my room I carried a dream and with it my green sweater, whose pocket held a package of donut seeds.

EPILOGUE

Letters from My "Warm Fuzzies" File

I taught from the heart to open the mind as the affective and cognitive domain merged into the realm called understanding, answering how, when, and most importantly why—why teach? We age, as kids and trees mark time. Trees get bigger, but each year I taught the same age of kids, keeping me young. Until of course, twenty to thirty years later time left its mark as these students sent their own children to "Mr. Abe's" class. Making learning fun, students remember how I made them feel. We must find ways to reach them—all of them. At times, before or after school students dropped in just wanting to talk, wanting advice. Having a true sense of self-worth, we knew who we were to each other; we were all connected with lives full of meaning, lives full of purpose. We were graciously included.

Gracious Inclusion moves from self to others and then back again. I am humbled by what I have meant to my students and their parents, but more so by what they have meant to me. Always putting students first, these notes and letters say: "Know me as a person, and I will learn the subject." But I would not know what I was really teaching them had they not told me. So beautiful is the character of the children and adults who have written them. Not asking, Gracious Inclusion happens.

•••

I Know You

Dear Mr. Abrahamson,

As one of your former students, I just wanted to thank you for making my son's school year more enjoyable for him. He isn't a kid that loves being at school, but having you for a teacher was one of the highlights of the year. Thank you for that! Have a great summer.

Sincerely,

J.L.

Mr. Abe—

You know you really caught me off guard on Friday afternoon. It took me a while to really realize what you said. I just want you to know, I really appreciate you. I don't think I realized how much I needed to hear everything you said. Just thank you so much for your support. Sometimes I think we talk ourselves into believing we don't need support. How wrong we are! Thank you for giving me that little boost I

160

needed. You are an outstanding teacher with a remarkable faith from what I could tell. You totally made my Friday and ultimately, you helped me see my goals a little differently.

Thank you and God bless! K

Mr. Abrahamson,

I would like to thank you in a most tremendously sincere way for helping me organize and relate my cluster of thoughts, ideas and philosophies into a basic outline. I will be filling in the paragraphs as I go through life. I must say that you are a buoyant, generous person in an ocean of greed.

Thanks again,

P

A Principal's Formal Classroom Observation

Mr. Abrahamson has discovered how vital it is to develop a positive rapport with his students before he can truly impact their academic development. He starts his lessons by greeting his students and asking questions that have more to do with getting to know them on a personal level than what it has to do with his science lesson.

He is compassionate about helping his students develop into responsible and caring young adults and realizes their need to experience success on a personal level. Dan truly understands what teaching our students is all about.

Signed respectfully,

S.A.

Making it Fun

Mr. Abrahamson,

Thank for helping me on homework and projects in Biology last quarter. Also, thank you for making the class so fun and complimenting me on my MMC paper. I'm glad you liked it. I appreciate and respect you for that. It's really amazing how you graded almost everything that same night and got it back to us the next day, even though you have your own life, it shows that you really care about us.

Thanks again, D

Mr. Abrahamson,

Never did I imagine that science could be so fun!! I enjoyed every moment of class time and loved the way you taught. You allowed your students to expand their own minds and didn't do it for them! I tell you—that is a true gift, and it will always be there.

R (P.S. I love science)

Dear Mr. Abrahamson,

I respect you because you are a teacher that knows how to have an extremely fun time in class while you still are teaching us about Biology. I also want to thank you for teaching at this school because if you didn't, I wouldn't have ever met you. Your class is the only class I look forward to in every day.

Sincerely, Ryan

P.S. "Bald is beautiful" Thank You for This Memory

Honored by Emulation

Mr. A

If I had to choose someone as my role model, it would you be you. You made the class fun. If I were to become a teacher, I would want to be like you. Even though I would never become a teacher, when I get a job, I hope I can make people happy as you do. J.R.

Mr. A,

This is D. N. I hope you remember me. It seems such a long time since I was in your Chem-Is-Try class. I just thought I'd drop you a line to say thank you for everything you taught me in high school. I'm so glad you taught at such an elevated level because I'm already way ahead of my Chemistry class here a UMD. Just in case you are wondering what my major is, it's Chemical Engineering and it's so much fun. My chemistry professor reminds me of you, except for his Russian accent. Being able to understand what is going on already helps. Thanks again for everything.

Sincerely, D.N.

P.S. "fire is still my best friend"

Kids Don't Want to Fail

Mr. Abe,

Thank you for all of your time and patience with me. Even when I give up, you don't. I don't know how I would survive a class like Chemistry without a teacher like you. I got so worried taking tests and never did well. But you found a way for me to show I did understand. It gives me extra motivation to know that you have faith in my potential.

Merry Christmas to you and your family,

K

Mr. A,

Thanks for giving me extra help and making me stick with Chemistry instead of failing.

T.H.

Liking the Class—A Stray Note Found on the Floor

Do you like Mr. Abrahamson's class? We do. W/B what's your favorite color?

Disgruntled Students Resist Not Being Spoon-Fed

(After asking students to make meaningful connections of their own
during the unit review, several students became resistant. The next day,
this note was attached to the back of a student's test.)

Mr. Abe,

I want to say that I'm sorry about what happened yesterday. I know I should have been a leader and said that we were taking it too far and I apologize for not doing so. I also know that some of the others are sorry too, but they will probably never say that.

I think that some are having a hard time with your teaching. You teach in a way that no other teacher does. And sometimes it's hard to understand you, so people get frustrated. That's one of the reasons we act the way that we do.

Well, I didn't want to enter the holiday season on a bad note. Again, I'm sorry and I hope that we can still get along better in the future. Have a Merry Christmas and a Happy New Year.

P.H.

A Card with a Baby Sea Turtle Crawling from the Beach into the Ocean

Dear Mr. Abrahamson

Thank you for writing such a great college recommendation letter for me! I was notified last Saturday that I have been accepted to go to Gustavus next fall. I'm really looking forward to going to college, but it's still scary to know that it's my last year of high school. Just like the baby sea turtles must leave the beach and go to the sea, I'm about to embark on a scary journey, but because you helped me, I have little to fear. Thank you for being such an amazing teacher! I'll try not to forget to email you in five years.

S

Empathy, an Emotional Attitude, the Driving Force of an Activated Amygdala

Mr. A,

This being my last lab report, I have mixed emotions. This obvious emotion is the happiness that arises from not having to write any more lab reports. The inner emotion is that of sorrow because I no longer get to participate in any of your fun-filled labs. I don't feel alone in my sorrow, however, because I know you're sad you don't get to see me next year. Don't be too sad, though, because my sister will be there in 3 more years to carry on the tradition of my family's excellence.

See ya! J

Mr. Abe,

My last two days of chemistry are here. It is crazy to think that I am done with high school forever. It is very bittersweet. I have learned so much, not only academically, but personally. I am sad to leave this small town with all my friends and family and move on to the big real world, but I'm excited to move on to bigger and better things.

I will always remember to "Be my best advocate" and I will always remember the inspiring man that taught me that! I will continue to Make Meaningful Connections. Thanks for everything. Good luck in the new high school.

K.D.

Made to Be Different

(My eccentricity became accepted, cherished, and protected as this student writes her own poem of recognition of self, the class, and me.)

<u>My Struggle</u>

We come to his class feeling shot
The chemistry room feels so hot
Sitting through class the month of May
His favorite movie is "Sandlot"

Lab reports pile up everyday
I'll get them done but not today
Pour acid in the tall clear flask
Don't spill on me or you will pay

He makes sure we all stay on task
"What are you doing?" He will ask
A new shirt he will never wear
He might as well just wear a mask

So, as you see I just don't care
Of how he walks or does his hair
He's unique and so very rare
But change my teacher, don't you dare!
K.K.

ACKNOWLEDGEMENTS

Thank you to:

My brother, Ben, for making my website, helping design the cover art and the Gracious Inclusion logo, and for being a sounding board; the eight principals, who over 36 years gave me guidance (even when I thought I didn't need it), entrusting me to be their extra pair of eyes and ears that reached far beyond the range of their office domain; Darrell, a fellow colleague, giving me a listening ear and then firing out a wise-crack to lighten my day; Karen, who was my co-worker and neighbor and so often times a travel-partner during inclement weather, late night parent-teacher conferences or whenever either of our cars broke down; Gene, seeing me from across the hallway as one lonely soul needing to be adopted into his crazy family when I was far from home; the camaraderie of so many other teachers, assistant principals and counselors, custodians, nurses, cooks, and secretaries who reacted to my growing eccentricity over the years by laughing with me and not at me.

To my wife and children:

You have seen this teacher coming home to be dad and husband...at times being hot-headed, but always having a soft heart, moving about a pivotal point that at best can be described as partly-cloudy. You've seen it all—the good and the bad. For at home there was nowhere to hide. What I taught you did not go in a book of lesson plans. Then as unbridled fireballs that lit darkened pages written long ago, you scribbled your own encrypted messages in a book that will be opened by future generations—you grew up. All wise before your age, you must have gotten your smarts from mom for it has taken me so long to figure things out.

And to my youngest daughter, Esther, Editor in Chief:

You were right, it is hard work writing from the inside out and storytelling is not sequential. You insisted on the removal of over-used clichés because you knew what I had inside of me was an original.

●●●

Thank you all for being on this journey with me. Children, both in and out of the classroom, will allow you to someday reflect on what you have been given. What is written will be read as we see ourselves in them.

ABOUT THE AUTHOR

Danny was born in Minnesota. A true homebody, he has lived there his entire life, except for briefly exploring Iowa during his first year of teaching. Dan and his wife, Kris, have four grown children, three of which have experiences of their own as teachers. Abe taught high school Biology, Chemistry, and Earth Space Science and retired from teaching in 2015 after 36 years in the classroom.

To learn more about the author and Gracious Inclusion please visit his website: www.graciousinclusion.com

Made in the USA
Monee, IL
25 May 2023